Mattole Press, San Francisco

Stained Glass from Mind to Light   An Inquiry into the Nature of the Medium   Narcissus Quagliata

Mattole Press
P.O. Box 22324
San Francisco, California 94122

ISBN 0916854-00-0
Library of Congress Catalog Number
76-10019

Edited by Gail Larrick
Design by Bruce Montgomery
Printed by Cal Central Press
Bound by Cardoza-James

To those whose language is dance. . .

. . .and little Orfeo

Contents

1 Introduction

3 Acknowledgements

7 Foreword

33 Chapter 1:
Basic Design

59 Chapter 2:
Elemental Sources

93 Chapter 3:
Seven Themes from Experience

137 Chapter 4:
Living with Glass

191 Chapter 5:
Five Artists in Stained Glass

242 Bibliography

Introduction

Narcissus Quagliata is an artist who came from Italy to study at the college of the San Francisco Art Institute. As he became a part of the community of artists in San Francisco, he undertook a personal exploration which carried him from the medium of painting to that of stained and leaded glass. True to a tradition which endures among artists here, he forged an untried path which led to the development of a highly personal form of expression. Beyond this, the creation of this book expresses in his way a spirit that is prevalent among many artists here: a concern for sharing, an openness that promotes positive results.

A significant part of the current movement of artists is the expansion of a supportive system; this is accomplished by educating new audiences, winning their interest, understanding, and, ultimately, their support. Narcissus learned from the medium of glass that it had the special qualities of tradition, visual brilliance and unfathomable possibilities; these qualities lend the medium to countless inventive public applications which introduce opportunities for cooperative work between artists, architects, craftsmen and the people of the community. From process to finished work of art, the glass work serves as a positive force and as a source of lasting inspiration and human expression. Narcissus' book shares an artist's experience and encourages others to develop their artistic abilities; ultimately the lives of millions of people will be touched.

Phil Linhares
Director of Exhibitions
San Francisco Art Institute
March, 1976

Acknowledgements

As I complete this book and make the final corrections, I realize that it was not created in a vacuum. Quite to the contrary, from conception to completion it was acted upon by so many people in so many different ways that I find it difficult to claim the authorship without some hesitation. For this reason I wish to include the names of those who have, in one way or another, made some contribution.

Though they were not directly involved in the creation of this book, I wish to thank my parents in Italy, especially my mother, for having sustained and encouraged my interest in art always, from the earliest age. Also in Italy I wish to thank my dear friends Professors Franco Serpa and Raffaele Romanelli for their shaping influences on my life. Professor Serpa's influence on my consciousness is so complete that I am quite sure I think or do nothing that does not bear his imprint in some way.

Full credit for the existence of this book should go to Ray Porter. It was his idea that this book be written, and his close and encouraging support gave me the stamina to work through all of the material in the last four years.

I am grateful to Marvin Mund, who introduced me to stained glass, and must thank Valery McKee, Rachel Mesrahi, Milton Newman, Jean Myers, and Jorge Schnitman, who have assisted me at some time or other in the making of many windows.

I thank Eva Jalkotzy, close friend and mother of my little son, Orfeo, who has assisted me throughout the making of this book, financially and emotionally.

The bulk of the text was written while I lived as a guest at Redwoods Monastery in northern California. These words are not enough to express the appreciation and gratitude I feel towards that community. The profound quiet and the meditative life there was such help to me while working. I am especially grateful to Mother Myriam and Sisters Diane and Veronique.

This book would not exist in the present form without the perceptive eye and shaping hand of Gail Larrick, who did more than just edit the material, but gave me useful criticism as I put it together, and of Bruce Montgomery, who designed the book and unified all of the information into one visual statement.

I also wish to express my appreciation and thanks to the warehouse community of Project One in San Francisco, where I live and have my studio, and especially Bill Kane who printed most of the photography for this book. My friends and neighbors have supported me in ways that range from emotional encouragement to making available their efforts and the various personal and technical resources that are here in the building.

I want to mention the useful presence and encouragement of many of my friends and their critical minds, particularly Joan Levinson, Jack Weller, Tron Bykle, Agatha Bennich Bykle, and Michael Piasecki.

I must thank another group of friends who effect and inspire my life by way of incantation, and whose talents I admire. They have danced patiently for me in my studio as I attempted to steal a bit of their souls by pursuing their shadows. Among them I must mention Neil Hassall, Cheryl McGuire, Abbigail Young, Erica Anderson, Varna Lohar-Singh, and Tom Ahern.

I am grateful to the painter Peter Holbrook for letting me use his beautiful photographs of flowers, grown by Talitha Glass, as source materials for designs in this book, as well as in my windows. And I want to thank architectural-designer Paul Widess and architect Lamberto Moris for contributing their work and ideas in the section on architecture.

A most important contribution to this book has been made by the five stained glass artists presented in Chapter 5:

Dan Fenton, Peter Mollica, Jeffrey Speeth, Paul Marioni, and Kathie Bunnell. I think this book would not be complete without the presence of their beautiful works and interesting thoughts.

Finally, a very special note of gratitude to Fred Martin, former director of the San Francisco Art Institute, who invited me to teach at the college and who has been responsive to my ideas concerning the use of glass as a relevant material for the creation of art today, and to Phil Linhares, who curated the first major exhibition of stained glass in the San Francisco Bay Area, recognizing the vitality of the work being done today in that medium.

Narcissus Quagliata
San Francisco
March, 1976

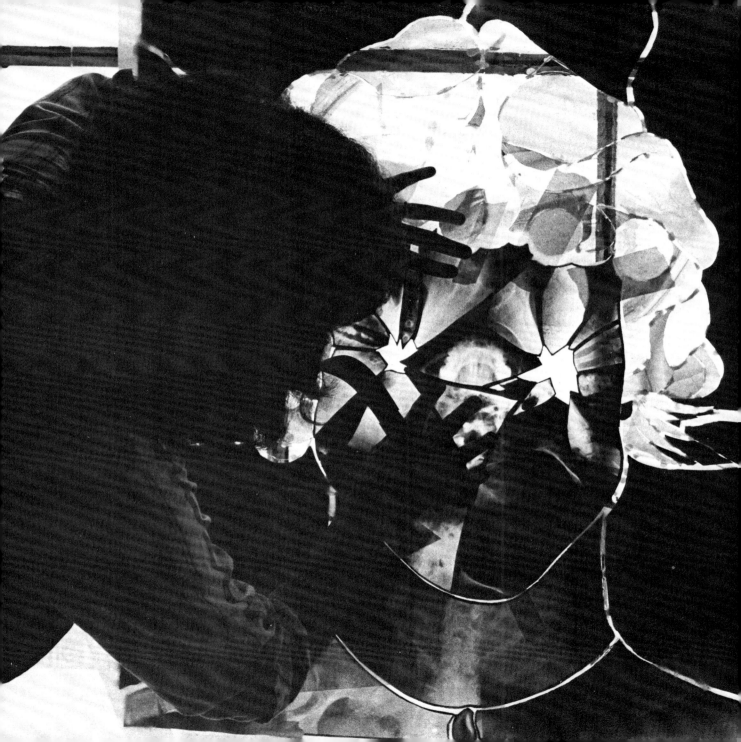

Foreword

I am attached to the notion that the expression of anything is possible with stained glass. View the medium as combining light and matter. Light melts, burns, and alters everything in its path, creating the profound excitement typical of stained glass works. Time shatters the glass, corrodes the lead and constantly acts on a window by way of the weather to change its appearance and remind us of its physical presence.

Beauty Is Function
The construction of a stained glass panel or a complete environment of glass raises the issue of whether living with beauty is a necessity. Stained glass can indeed be a luxury, and a beautiful one at that! But if we feel that at its core life is concerned with the perception of what is meaningful or what may be beautiful, then the function of stained glass changes, because it allows the perception of light to become a vital and important experience.

Stained glass is a medium at the beginning of its history, full of unexplored possibilities and uses. Most people still associate with stained glass the feeling of something mysterious and ancient. I seek in this book to reverse that feeling by emphasizing what is new, what is possible, what has barely begun. I wish to introduce a new awareness of stained glass that will not box it into definitions but will stimulate us into redefining and rediscovering the potentials innate in stained glass and in its use.

Glass: Blower's Pipe to Installation
If you're interested in stained glass, don't stop at the aesthetic experience of the finished work, but understand the material as well. Develop a feeling for those who work with it and those who use it. Visit the factories where glass is made. Such firsthand experience will make you appreciate the material at its birth. The journey of glass from raw material to refined work is revealing.

In Germany today interesting stained glass work, designed by master designers and executed in independent studios, is produced primarily for buildings. The character of some of the German work is overwhelming because of the large size of the panels and because it functions in direct relationship to the architecture that contains it. The human figure as a main theme and passionate concern is conspicuously absent. Reproductions of the works of stained glass artists such as Ludwig Schaffrath, Franz Nagel and Georg Meistermann are available, and I urge you to view them.

In the United States, on the other hand, and primarily in California, a large number of stained glass works are created by individual artists who construct their windows themselves. Some of their work is installed in houses, some in public places, but a large portion remains in the form of independent panels. These panels are interesting because they are a very pure form of painting, using light as the medium, and at the same time they are an inquiry into glass as a medium with its own laws, qualities and uses, quite different if not outright the opposite of painting. These panels are occasionally shown in galleries; they function partially as windows, partially as transparent artwork. My own work has grown out of this atmosphere and I speak from this viewpoint.

A Meeting Point
Artists in other mediums have sometimes been drawn to stained glass by the desire to work with color at the peak of its intensity. Eventually (unless the work is limited only to small panels), making stained glass windows forces the artist to consider the use of the work. Because of their easy mobility, it is feasible to paint a series of very large canvases, but to construct a stained glass piece as large as a wall without having considered a place for its installation is expensive and somewhat absurd. Without proper light, it cannot even be seen! The issue of use begins to force a rethinking of our relationship to our environment and consequently to our culture.

Creative people have an ambiguous love-hate relationship to our times. On the one hand, they harbor resentment towards a culture that has the capacity to instrumentalize everything, including art, into a product, which deadens its true meaning. On the other, they are responsive to the unquestionably charged and exciting atmosphere in the art and media world and long to end their estrangement and be integrated so as to share in its life, affluence and power. If we feel the genuine desire to live in a less repressive and truly liber-

ated society with changed values, we must first of all wage a political battle that begins against ourselves. The "bourgeois society" is apparent not only in its more obviously identifiable exterior manifestations, but inside our studios; its values permeate our work and tint our expectations. Why do we create artwork? For ourselves? For other people? For "the people"? As a way to pass time playfully? To become famous? As a joke? To what degree is our work a creative contribution to our time that would be as valid to us if it were anonymous?

Seemingly, in the last hundred years, artists and architects have lived at completely opposite poles. Artists working in the fine arts have existed outside the mainstream of culture, while practicing architects worked within the culture, experiencing on a daily basis the problems and contradictions of our times. The result of this complete parting of the ways has been a virtual end to dialogue between the visual arts and architecture. The public has suffered the loss. The lack of dialogue has meant a loss of value to the architecture itself, but has also created a lack of any meaningful visual input by contemporary artists into many structures built recently. I believe the dialogue between artists and architects is finally beginning again.

Stained glass is a perfect medium of experimentation for artists interested in integrating their work into actual environments and in going beyond their private studio experience. For architects it serves as a way to bring more color, more playfulness, more meaning into their buildings and to utilize the resources of contemporary artists.

The Function of Beauty
I believe that, for the artist, the object of creating artwork is primarily twofold: to create a dialogue between himself and life via the medium (a philosophical activity), and to communicate. Natural light is an effective means of communication because it is primal and essential to all who are alive. No education is required to be able to respond to its beauty and be truly moved by it. I view stained glass as a perfect means to focus on light itself, to bring our attention to it and to make it acutely perceptible in much the same way that a crystal prism breaks down a ray of sunshine to make all its colorful components visible.

I view using stained glass as an opportunity to draw extremely close to the viewer, addressing ourselves to the "person" at the core, beneath the cloth-ing of taste and social class. Ultimately the value of the medium, when used well, lies in its incredible ability to produce profound and primal pleasure.

Most of the visual information in this book is conveyed in photographs of finished works and cartoons, schematic in character. The cartoons—the working visualizations or patterns for the windows—illustrate the middle point when the ideas are formed yet still full of possibilities for expansion. The photographs show the end result. A few sketches are also included, where relevant, to reveal the beginning of an idea.

To create a window for every idea I wished to include in this book would have been impossible. I have created cartoons that you, the reader, may liberate with your imagination beyond their limited black-and-white reality. I invite you to use this book as a coloring book. Color the cartoons to your liking.

Some cartoons are complete and could be executed by cutting glass to the pattern. To reveal the image implied by others, the use of painting, etching, or sandblasting would be necessary. Some cartoons are still in flux. They are intended to represent a direction, an idea, and could be simplified or made more rich and complex. If they serve as stimulus, you may complete them in your own way. Some of the cartoons have been printed in reverse as negatives. The purpose of this printing was to point to the different atmospheres possible with the same design through the use of a reversal of light and dark glass.

Working with black-and-white renderings where a surface should be alive with color and light was difficult. Though the presentation is stark, the graphic quality of the designs is more direct and available. I feel I had to skin stained glass of the flesh to get to the bones.

Some designs should be viewed as attempts to reflect a state of mind in precarious balance between literary connotations, allusions to other forms, and simply design of glass and lead. Within the medium of stained glass, infinite design possibilities are available. Only a few have been explored.

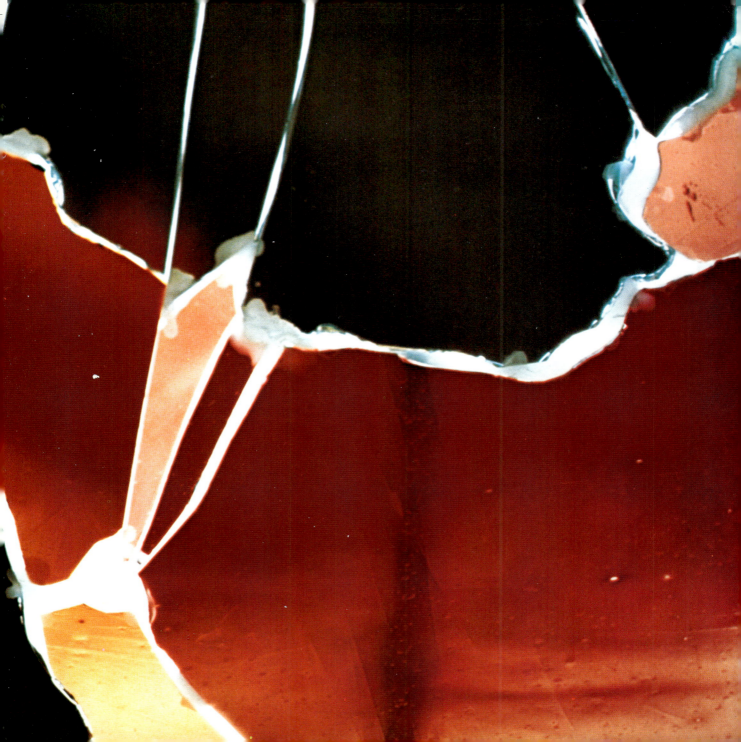

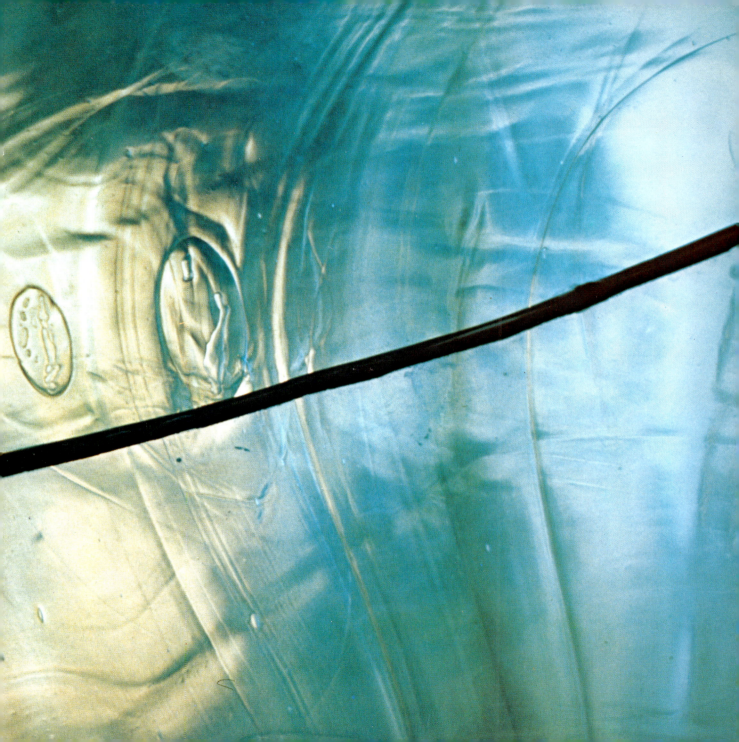

1

2

3

4

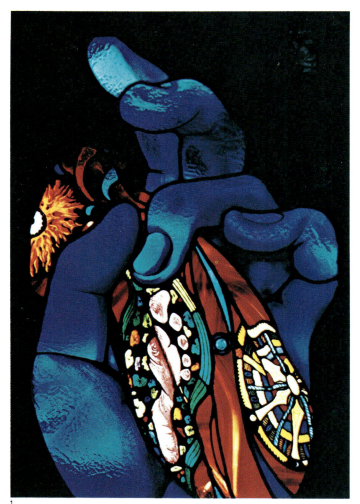

Narcissus Quagliata, *Narcissus Series:*
1. *Birth,* 1970, 36″×44″.
2. *Transformation,* 1970, 36″×44″.
3. *Death,* 1970, 36″×44″.
4. *The Tantrum,* 1971, 36″×44″.

1. Narcissus Quagliata, *Blue Buddha Hand,*
   1971, 27″×41″, San Francisco Zen Center.
2. Narcissus Quagliata, *The Rice Bowl,* 1971,
   32″×44″, Soto Zen Monastery, Tassajara Hot
   Springs, California.

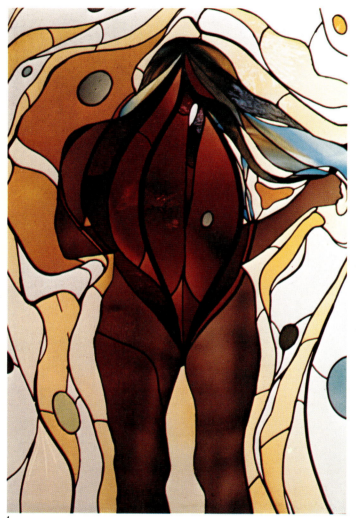

1

2

1. Narcissus Quagliata, *Eva*, 1975, 4′ × 6′.
2. Narcissus Quagliata, *My Androgynous Shadow*, 1975, 46″ × 72″.
3. Narcissus Quagliata, *Stained Glass Suicide*, 1975, 4′ × 6′.

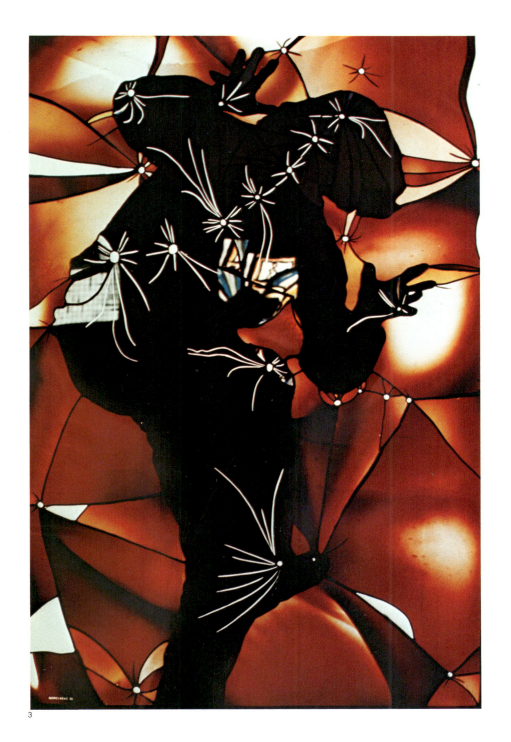

2

3

1. Narcissus Quagliata, watercolor design for six-paneled stained glass screen, *Dancing, Dancing, Dancing . . . San Francisco Cabaret, 1972-1975*, 1975, 7' × 12'.

2–13. Narcissus Quagliata, *Reflection House*, San Francisco, 1975.

4

5

6

7

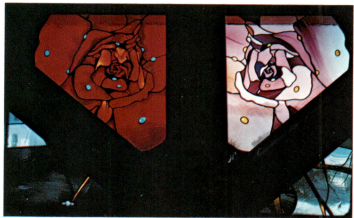

8

9

10

11

12

13

1

The Cartoon

When you think of a good idea for your window, don't rush its execution. You need not fix it in great detail right away. Let it linger on the page incomplete, let it grow on you. Live with the idea for a while. Then, when you know your feelings are truly and fully represented by that image, close in on it decisively. Otherwise, you might draw the pattern for the window in great excitement and begin a window, seeing its shortcomings only later when it will be too late for change. Making a window takes a bit of time.

Working on a design to define where the lead lines go is like setting up the armature for a sculpture. In a sculpture, the armature is support—it holds the piece up; it is essential. Later it will disappear from sight. Lead in a window is very much the same. Your eyes tend to perceive only the glass, in most cases.

Don't begin your window unless your lead design is clear and expressive of your idea. If your lead design is weak, the color of the glass and the subsequent painting, if that is to be added, will not correct this initial weakness.

Do not rush through the designing so you can handle the glass right away. Spend time on your cartoon. The cartoon itself, unembellished by color, must be an already strong, clear presence.

The Image

An image in stained glass may be created in two basic ways. The image may be defined by chunks of color (like a mosaic) and their gradation or contrast, or you may let the lead describe it. In the first method the lines are but a necessary structure so that the colors may be next to each other; in the second, the lead lines themselves form the image and as such take on a more expressive and descriptive role than that of being only structural.

When you draw the cartoon in preparation for a window, don't be inhibited by the thought that the lines will eventually become lead. Whether your design is representational or abstract, it will be most vivid if it includes a variety of lines, different in thickness and character from each other. Be aware of the many different types of line you can draw—draw first a curvy flowing line, a jagged line, then a soft but forceful line. Do some exercises if you need to. How many types of line you can create? Think of adjectives to characterize your lines. Are they funny or obsessed or unpredictable? Consider whether your lines effectively express the moods you decide upon. Think of line not just as the edge of something, separating shapes from one another, but also as a path, an energy flow, motion—like a trail of ants.

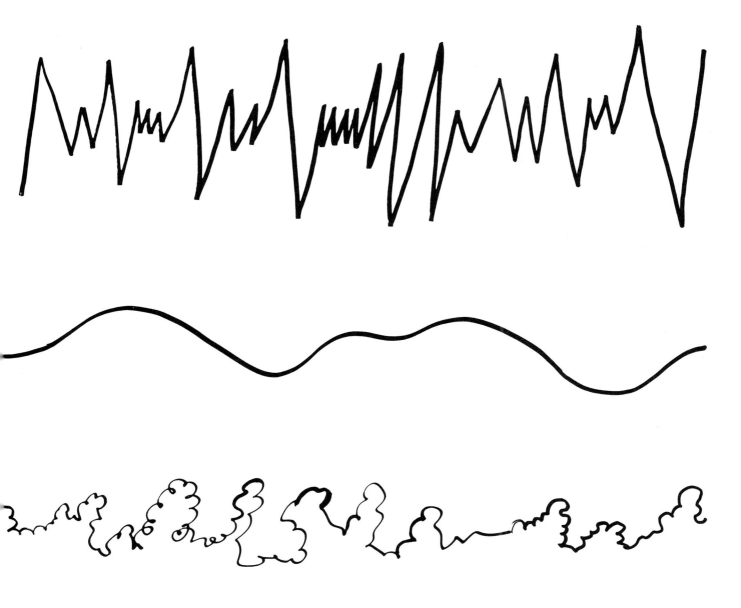

The Use of Line

Because the drawn lines on a cartoon must eventually become lead lines and contain glass between them, and because they define space, an image may be flat or in perspective on the picture plane. To show what can be done with lead lines, I have drawn some examples which I hope will be useful to you in designing your own work. A line need not always be the same in width but can increase or decrease as you splice different thicknesses of lead together while glazing the window. And, depending on how you do it, the lead line can grow or diminish gradually or in steps. Superimposition of one image on top of another is a very effective means of designing a cartoon with tension and originality. View the same image in perspective, and understand that a whole window can be made along the lines of a visual illusion.

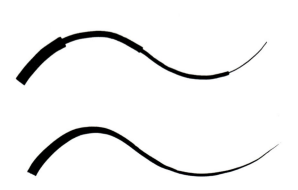

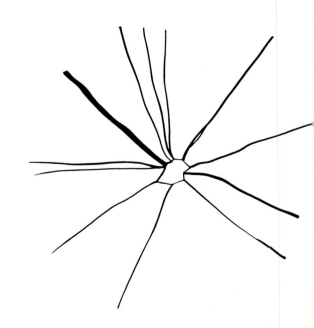

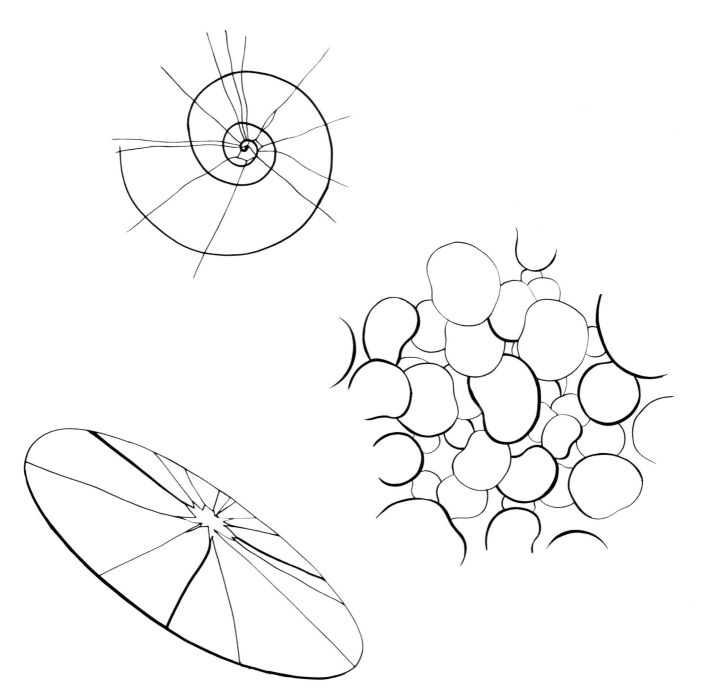

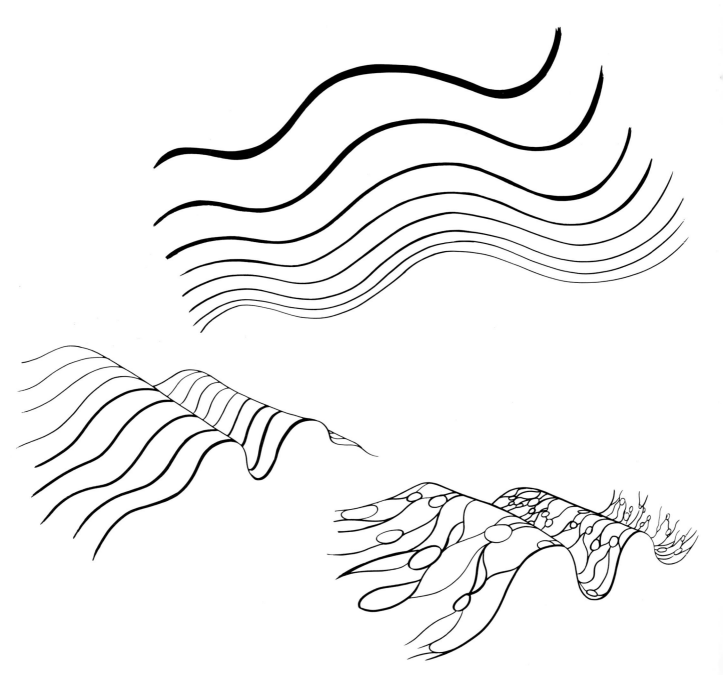

The Lead Lines

Lead lines can define planes, and create a feeling of shallow but layered space by use of overlapping edges and variation in the line thickness. Lines of different thicknesses may be used next to each other. Depth of field can be achieved by the proper use of the line's direction and emphasis on thickness. The overall effect is one of looking at a carpet in the wind. Parallel lines form strands of glass that can be braided together, going behind and in front of each other.

Notice parallel strands of equal strength and their visual effect, much like an energy band moving across a field.

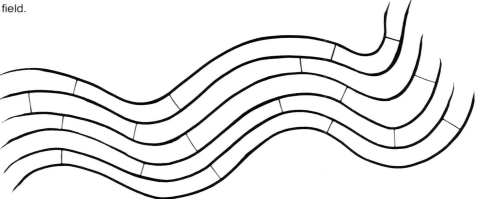

Motion backwards in space can be achieved by braiding glass pieces or creating a series of discs (that might be different shapes as well) and making them gradually recede. Finally, lines can define tubular motion through space. This concept is especially useful in creating the stem of any organic form. These examples are presented to counter the commonly held belief that a window should be flat, like a carpet hanging on the wall. With the use of line only, and without the help of color, you can make the picture plane come out, recede or undulate to your liking.

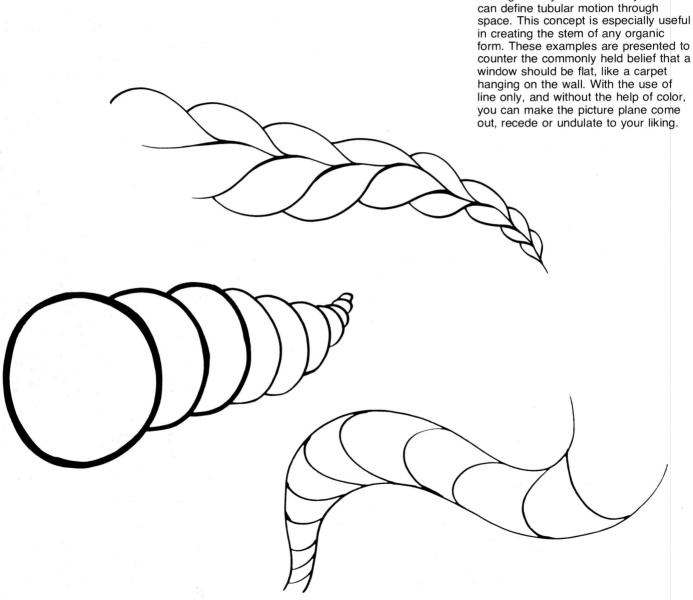

Your First Project

Because your first project is your first experience with stained glass design, do your best, but don't expect too much from your cartoon image or from the end result. The purpose of your first project is not to make a "beautiful piece" immediately, but to acquaint you with the feel of the medium. Experience the glass and how it breaks, experience the lead and how it solders, and learn the waterproofing process. Then, once you grasp the process from beginning to end, you are truly ready to begin your creative work.

A series of design and windows, all first attempts designed by beginning students at the college of the San Francisco Art Institute in the summers of 1972 through 1975 follow. These projects might give you an idea of various possibilities and directions that are available from the offset.

Six cartoons based on first design attempts by beginning students.

42

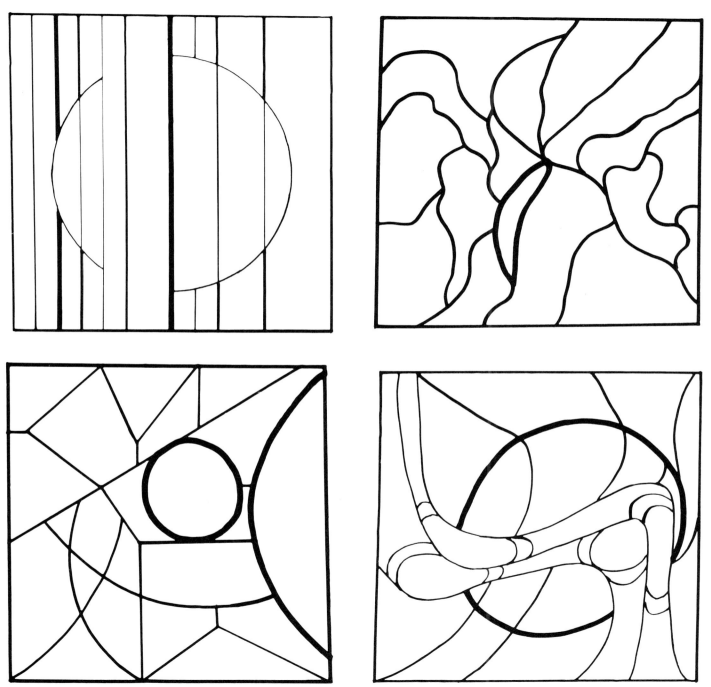

43

1

Six first projects executed in glass:
1. Christine Reinhold.
2. Roxanne Quimby.
3. Alan Silver.
4. Dan Gulyban.
5. Karen Johnson.
6. Kathleen Pittman.

4

2

3

5

6

45

Your Second Project

You have struggled through your first experience and are either ready to quit altogether or to try again, with the feeling that you can take on a much more complex project. This time allow yourself to design a rather ambitious window. Test yourself by doing a work at the very limit of your ability. The tension of never quite knowing if you can handle the project will keep you alert and interested.

Following are reproductions of some second projects done by students in the same classes. Notice that in their second attempt the students are capable of expressing the flavor of a much more personal vision, in some cases humorous, in other cases lyrical. All these windows are no smaller than one-and-a-half-foot square and no larger than three-foot square.

1

1. Alan Sonneman
2. Alan Silver
3. Elise Keely

2

3

4

5

4. Mary Lake.
5. Arden Simpson.
6. Irene Koch.
7. Pamela Brown.

6

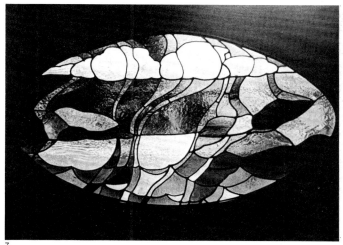

7

8. Dede Duckworth.
9. Diane Gray.

8

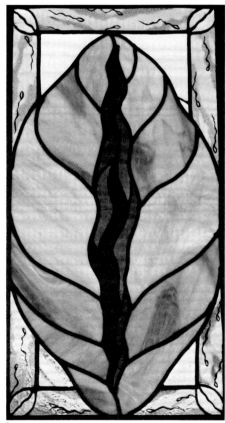

9

Color

Color is to a window what skin is to a body; it's what you most readily see. But the light you perceive through glass is much more than surface. It is the soul of the glass, or the heart of it. In this context I do not wish to make any lengthy analysis of solar light. Those interested should look for various other books on the subject, and many exist. I only wish to be of aid to a beginner choosing bits of glass to make a first window.

If your window is to be installed in a predestined place, your problems will be very specific, and the range of glass colors you can choose from narrows.

Deep colors—purples, greens, deep reds, and the like—will vibrate to the fullest only if the inside space from which you view them is dark and the outside is bright. If your window is lit almost exclusively from the outside, light will be rushing through your panel, giving it force and vitality. Consider that light is like water, barely contained in a dam. If at the bottom of the dam you open just a small aperture, the water will rush through with tremendous power. In a dark environment, the window to the outside is just that very aperture. A window interposed to that rush of light will benefit from all of that energy.

If your window instead divides a bright inside from an only slightly brighter outside, the choice of colors is reduced. That situation confines you to clear and light tints, since deeper colors will tend to become inky. To use the same comparison as before, light is like water spilling from a full pool into a slightly lower one with ease, without a great rush. The energy transfer is less violent.

Color in glass is unlike color on white paper. When you make a stained glass window you add the element of transparency.

The same color may be found in a transparent sheet of glass and in a more opaque one. If you like the background behind the window you'll be constructing, use transparent glass to incorporate it into your work. If you wish to block it out, use opal glass, which acts much like a veil, holding the light to make you aware of its surface.

If your window is to be an independent panel, you will choose the glass in relationship to the other parts of the panel. Only when the window is complete will you look for an appropriate place in which to set it. The whole spectrum of possibilities is open to you, from clear window glass to deep tones in blown glass. You need only make sure your choices relate well to each other.

Clear glass is used very often, especially antique clear. The glass is beautiful and extremely useful. Clear glass is like frozen water, a thin and transparent sheet of ice, refreshing. Its usefulness comes from its subtle presence in a window. It does not jump out at you, but gently draws you in and is like a field of crystal on which other colors can float.

Blown clear glass comes in varying degrees of reaminess (irregular waves in the glass) or seediness (bubbles in the glass).

When you use a large quantity of clear glass, the background becomes part of the piece. Be aware of the character of the background and its effect on your glass composition. By using different varieties of clear glass in your window, the background (be it a grove of trees or the brick building next door) will come alive because of varying degrees of distortion and clarity.

I have seen very little black nontransparent glass being used. I have enjoyed using black glass very much. Its properties and possible uses are interesting. If it surrounds a deep-colored glass, such as a deep blue or purple, it will make the deep colors appear bright, and give them vibrancy and that "magic glow" often ascribed to stained glass. As a background to a very complex image, black glass will make the image appear to float suspended in space and glow unimpaired by a background. Its essence is anti-light, and this quality is what makes this glass so fascinating. Black glass in a window makes you aware of it as "body," as "reality" in contrast to illusion. Black glass refuses to be transformed or transfixed. I admire its stubbornness.

In making a window, we must decide first of all what kind of a presence —vigorous or subtle—the window is meant to have. The primary colors used to their fullest radiance suggest primal thoughts and emotions, while the effectiveness of a window of tints and greys is more in its capacity to capture mood and atmosphere.

Six different types of glass.

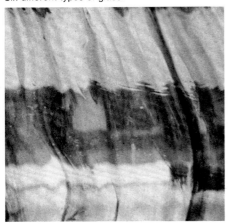

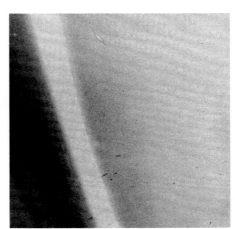

Color, and especially color in glass, carries with it an intrinsic symbolic meaning. This is said to be so because of our instinctive associations between color and the realm of nature. To blue and purple are ascribed powerful religious and spiritual connotations, to yellow an intellectual character, to red the association with life itself, and to green the quality of harmony and naturalness.

I don't deny such associations. When we see blue, we certainly think more often of the sky than of blood, and when we see red, we think of fire and blood before the sky. What interests me is not so much the expression of color in its already obvious, known, symbolic content, but the creative discovery of color anew, over and over again. Colors exist, each one with its different character, like alchemical substances. Each one remains a mystery, ready to be mixed in a myriad of combinations to reveal more fully its own intrinsic nature, as well as thoughts and perceptions of it which have never yet been expressed.

From a purely optical standpoint, you should be aware that each colored glass does behave differently when perceived through a square aperture in a dark wall. Blue will soften at the outer edge of the square and expand. It is, in part, this phenomenon that gives blue glass that magic glow. Red, too, will act on the square's edge, but will slightly contract it. Yellow will keep the square's shape perfectly, while white (not to be confused with clear glass) will tend to emphasize the square's pointed corners, making them appear slightly sharper.

Mirrored glass (one-or two-way) is even harder to discuss than colored glass. The ways it can act in a window or environment are almost countless. Placed in a bright window against the light, it will function as a dark spot, but as the surface light in the space inside increases, it will slowly pull into the window the reality of what's inside and merge it with the glow of the images of what's outside.

Such glass can be tricky and easily used as a gimmick, but it can also be very beautiful. Paul Marioni uses this mirror effect very well in his "Cadillac" (see Chapter 5).

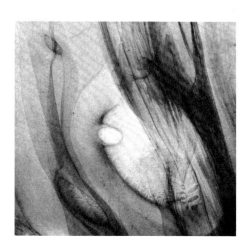

Light

The early morning light from the east is lemon-crisp and delicate. It seems barely to touch the physical environment. As the day progresses to noon, and differently on each day of each season, the direct sunlight seems to create an atmosphere of stasis, no change, especially in the summer. Finally, in the late afternoon, the light pours into the windows like a ripe and rich orange stream, tired and so beautiful.

A stained glass window exists because of light—it *is* light through the vehicle of glass. As such, the window fully partakes in the day since it appears at sunrise and fades after sunset.

When we install a window, it can face only one direction. Since the light from each of the four cardinal directions has a unique cycle of its own, it will act on the window in a very specific way. To understand light's effect on the glass we wish to use is crucial, in order to avoid surprises and unwanted effects after the window is complete.

From the east and the southeast, the direct morning light is so crisp and cool that we can interpose any color, warm or cool, without it becoming too strong. Reds and oranges will come to life and have a vivid effect.

Reds and oranges faced to the west and southwest will look fine in the morning in the indirect light. In the afternoon, a primarily red and orange window penetrated by warm rays will become so vibrant and strong as to reach almost the limit of vulgarity—an effect which may be intended or desired. A window in strong warm colors facing west tends to overexpose and bleach out much like a slide, whereas blues, greens and greys vibrate to their fullest in the same exposure.

6 am

noon

3 pm

A window facing north is not exposed to direct sunlight, and therefore does not undergo as dramatic a change throughout the day as it would if it were facing south. Any color, skillfully used, will ring clear and not become overbearing in this light.

These general observations are not to be taken as rules. Absolutely no rules are fixed when it comes to a creative use of light. Every situation is different; every work attempts a different effect.

I suggest you select a set of given colors you like in sheets of glass. Observe them throughout a full day facing north, south, east, and west to see for yourself the changes they go through.

A stained glass window is completely dependent on circumstances for its appearance. It is subject to changes because of the hour of the day, the season, the exposure, the background behind it, because the weather is sunny or foggy, because of the specifics of its installation. If you leave it leaning against a wall, it is a physical presence, grey and inert.

The "window" does not exist outside of the specific circumstances it is immersed in. I must wait for days to experience my windows in my favorite light—that light I feel makes them live to the fullest.

Finally, see a window as a three-dimensional streak of light in space, if it is facing the sun. The light coming through the window is an extension of it that colors the environment and quietly moves to tint the floors, the walls and the objects in its path.

7 pm

9 pm

midnight

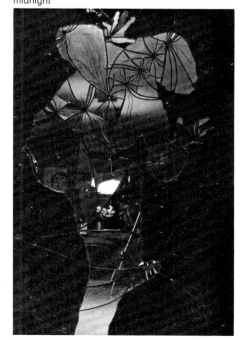

Glass

When buying your glass, notice each sheet not only for the color but for other qualities as well. Every sheet of blown glass is unique. See if the glass has any texture at all, study the texture, pick out interesting defects, such as bubbles. You can use them in strategic places in your design, for highlights.

Rolled glass feels very different from blown, or antique glass. Even among antique glass, a world of difference exists between, for example, German, French, English and American glass. A sensitive maker of windows develops the ability to put together pieces of glass that relate in a meaningful way, and not only with regard to color, but also texture and smoothness.

Traditional Treatments

A window can be made by using only glass, cutting it and glazing it, or by adding the step of altering the glass with various methods, and then glazing it together.

Traditional techniques of working on the glass include *painting.* Adding black or brown paint gives each piece more definition, after the glass is fired to fix the paint on it. You must realize the color is provided by the glass itself, so all you can add is some shading, molding or detail.

Silverstaining involves painting the glass with silver nitrate stains which, after the glass is properly fired, will rub off and leave a yellow to orange stain.

Etching is a way of biting through flashed glass to the clearer core, allowing a single piece of glass to be at the same time colored and clear.

All these techniques can be used on the same piece of glass, if desired, to give it a very rich elaborate look. You should know, however, that a standing debate continues about whether it is better to leave the glass untouched or paint on it and fire it before glazing. On the one hand, some say that a window is more beautiful if the glass is not treated, but rather used in the way the blower leaves it, in its purest form. This glass has maximum brilliance and sparkle. These debaters say painting alters the glass through the firing. A window wants to be a window, and if the painted illusion by way of alteration of the glass pushes it beyond this point, it will fight against the very grain of the material of which it's made.

On the other hand, it can be said that painting refines a window. Painting can indeed give the window more of the quality of being an "illusion," but this quality is not a weakness. Painting multiplies the visual possibilities of glass almost to infinity. It can make of a circle of glass a sphere, of an oval an expressive face.

Personally I don't lean in either direction because I feel both approaches to be completely sound; good works come out of both paths.

Painting on glass.

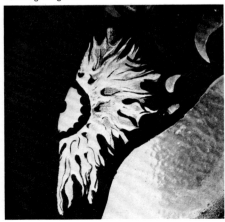
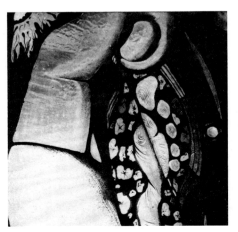
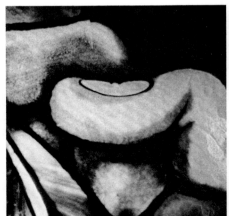

Newer Techniques

In recent years several new techniques have emerged to alter the character of the medium and enlarge its potential.

Photosilkscreen. The transfer of a photographic image onto glass is now possible by screening the image directly onto the surface with glass paint, then fixing it by firing, or etching it in. The potential of this technique is unlimited, since it pulls into the palette of the maker of windows the whole world of photography. Photography, a whole art form with its own history, tradition and meaning, can produce interesting single panels when combined with stained glass (see Paul Marioni's "Lady in Waiting," Chapter V), as well as large transparencies of environmental proportions. However, work on combining these two mediums has barely begun. The field is wide open.

Judy Raffael is successfully working with this process. An example of her work with the technique can be seen in the doors of the Salvation Army Chapel at 1450 Powell Street, San Francisco, California.

Sandblasting and Carving Glass. A sandblaster is a very valuable tool in a stained glass maker's studio. With it you can remove the flash from the surface of the glass replacing the traditional technique of acid etching, or you can put a light frost on the surface of the glass. The tool can also carve into the glass itself at different depths to form interesting images, as well as blast right through it to form holes where other colored pieces of glass can be inserted without the support of lead lines going to them. Finally, with a sandblaster you can shape a piece of glass in a way that you could never do with a glasscutter and pliers. Again, Paul Marioni has made excellent use of this technique (see Chapter 5).

Mr. Kaye Warren is a master glasscarver. He is singlehandedly responsible for making many artists in the San Francisco Bay Area, including Paul Marioni and Kathie Bunnell and others, aware of what sandblasting used with skill can do for their work. Many glass artists visit his colorful shop in San Francisco to ask him for assistance in some form or other. I enjoyed visiting him and listening to him talk about carving glass. He showed me many of his virtuoso pieces. Then, showing me an incredibly delicate animal shape he had carved out, he pointed out to me that in his opinion the existence of a sandblaster transforms what a window can be altogether, and makes traditional window design obsolete. "With a sandblaster you can make a glass puzzle and then glaze it!"

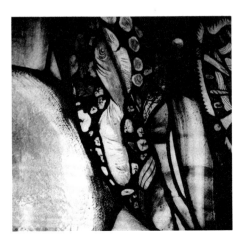
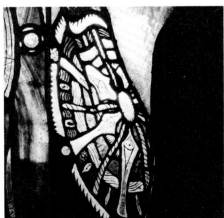

Thoughts on Working

Laminating. Laminating flattened objects between two thin pieces of glass is also a possibility to keep in mind. Anything you can squeeze in can also be glazed in! You can then add to your visual vocabulary X-rays, pressed plants, feathers, lace and anything flat and semi-transluscent. The insertion of an object into your glass can add a fetishlike quality to the window.

Next to the freshness and immediacy of working with watercolors, stained glass feels heavy and clumsy. The time that elapses between conception and completion is so long! The windows are heavy, and they do break easily if they are not handled properly. Stained glass is soft and gentle like light itself, once in place, but also so heavy and brittle!

I believe that only if you bring to the glass the richness of your emotional and intellectual life, your fear of death, your hidden or obvious lust, your most tender moments, or any one of these in full, can you then begin.

Yet glass is glass and it wants to be itself. It should be treated and respected as itself. It is necessary to forcefully design a window in great detail, but it is just as necessary to surrender and be sensitive to the way the material wants to exist.

Keep in mind, don't be so serious when you work. Be relaxed, be playful!

Sandblasting through glass.

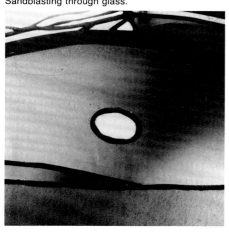

Sandblasting mirroring.

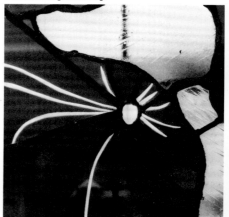

2

Introduction

Within this chapter, I am introducing
themes which have been dear to me. In
some instances I show various stages
of a design to reveal its development.
And I will explain why I chose the subject and what particular fascination it
has for me. From my sleep, as a counterpoint, comes a dream image for each
theme.

Flowers

Flowers preceded us on Earth. They have been with us and meant something to us from the beginning of time. They serve countless functions in our personal and social customs.

We place them in our hair, on tables, on altars. We give each other flowers to express our feelings. Artists have used flowers as symbols for many human experiences and qualities: purity, passion, martyrdom, and sexuality.

I like flowers, so I often use them in my work. Stained glass expresses well their essential quality. The variety of colors and tints in flowers can be matched with the variety of colors and shades in glass. Glass, up against the light, becomes alive and recreates in its own way the quality of flowers.

The following illustrations of simple, complex and negative cartoons suggest alternatives to the all-too-often exploited art nouveau flower designs. The initial basic image is achieved by transfer from a slide. I elaborate or simplify the image to my taste.

Dream: Walking in a green field I saw a California poppy in the grass. It was black instead of yellow. Slowly I understood the poppy was not in the grass but inside my pupil. I watched it grow and grow until it blackened my whole field of vision.

Calendula

Nasturtium

California poppy

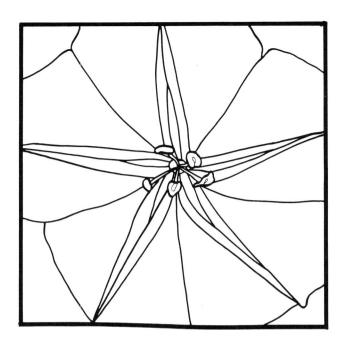

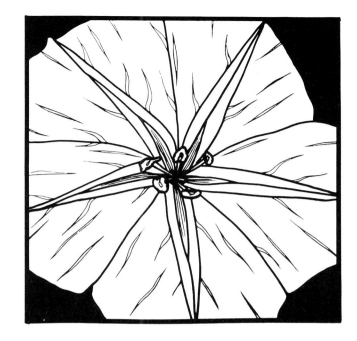

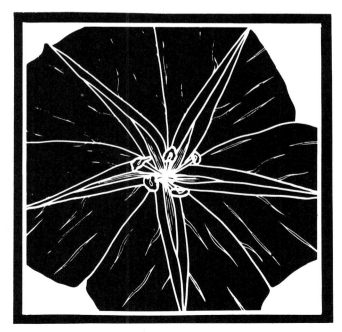

Morning glory

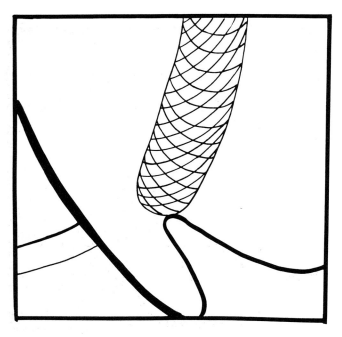

Anthurium

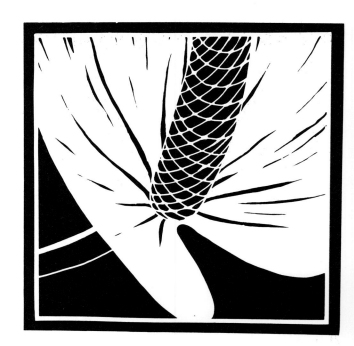

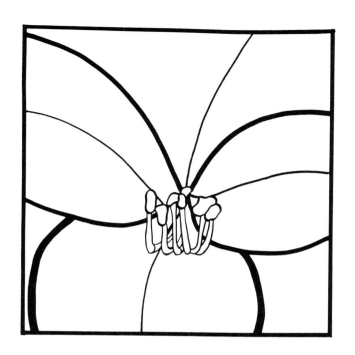

Hippeastrum

Crocus

Geranium

Water and Water Reflections

The themes of water and reflections are very dear to me. I think first of all of the affinity of water and glass; one reminds you of the other.

Looking into a pool of water along a creek is a complex experience. Right away you notice the body of water, cool and transparent, moving or still. On its glossy surface you'll see the trees, the sky and the reality around you. The temptation to lean over and look at oneself is almost irresistible.

But whatever you see reflected looks like a dream image of your surroundings. This image is upside down and vertically penetrates the water; it defies the feeling of just resting on its surface. Through this reflection you will see appear the forms of the bottom; that, too, is a whole world in itself. The creek bottom can be rich with different stones and pebbles of all sizes and color.

Finally your eye may catch sight of a fish or a whole school swimming through, and you can feel their organic presence.

These worlds penetrate into each other playfully, fade in and out of each other, and to me are a beautiful symbol of the multidimensional quality of the human mind. These illustrations are cartoons in various stages of completion for stained glass windows on the subject of water and water reflections.

Dream: Floating on the surface of the sea, facing the blue daylight sky, a cut begins forming on my body, lengthwise. A vagina opens me up, parts me in two, and it keeps opening 'till I can see the night sky through it and below me. As if sucked by the vacuum, the sea water begins rushing through me, falling toward the stars below, dissipating in the void.

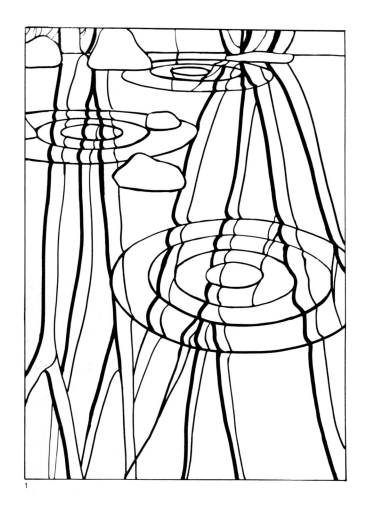

1

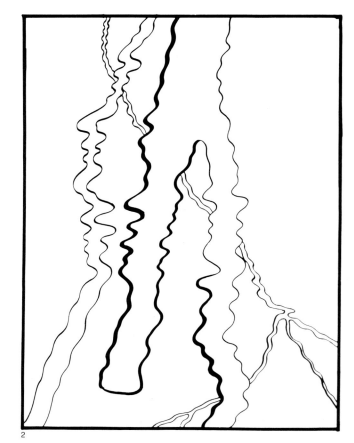

2

1. Cartoon: A reflection on water.
Three stages of making a cartoon:
2. First impression.
3. Further development.
4. The completed cartoon.

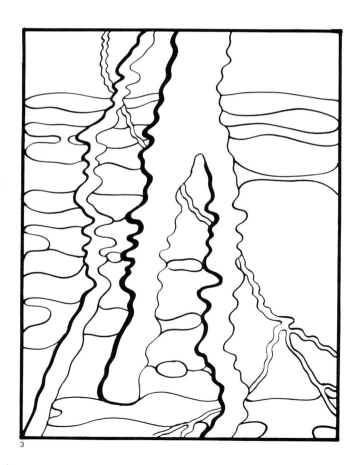

3

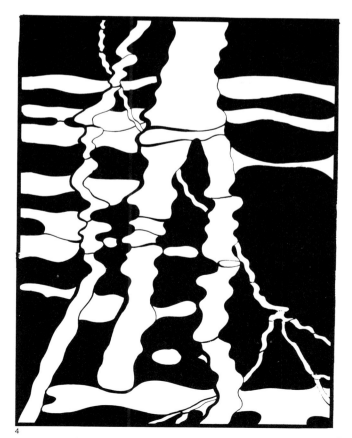

4

1

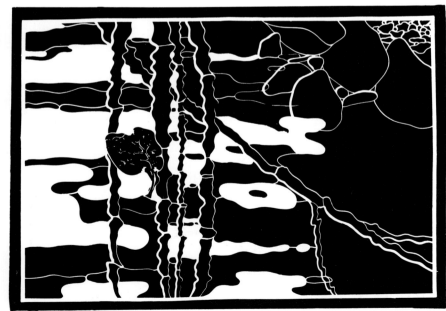

2

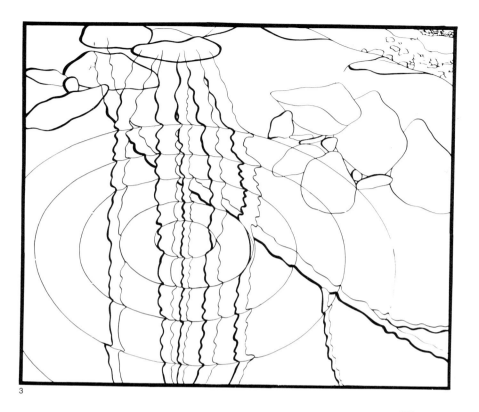

3

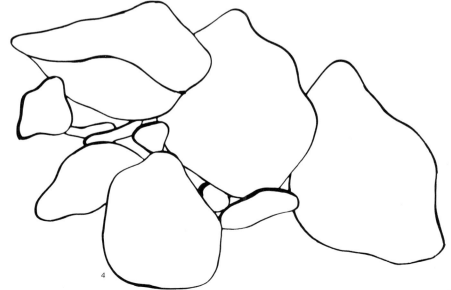

1. Completed cartoon: Reflections.
2. Negative print.
3. Cartoon with ripples.
4. Detail.

4

1

1. Cartoon: Swift moving water.
2. Cartoon: Water through narrow crevace.
3. Cartoon: Water around a rock.

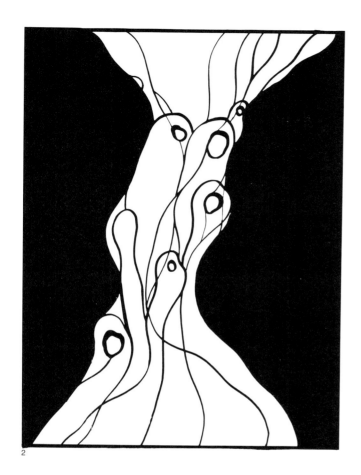

2

3

Fire

Fire always fascinates me; it keeps me in a state of hypnosis when I really look at it. Fire has the uncanny ability to reveal the structure of something in the very process of consuming it. A building on fire shows its structure much like bones before collapsing altogether.

During the winter of 1973 I made a series of watercolors by directly looking into the fire. These few cartoons are derived from those watercolors. They are limited in scope and purpose, but I hope they reveal a glimpse of what that powerful all-consuming energy can do in a glass design.

Dream: I remember being crouched on the ground, my knees and elbows drawn together, my head between my hand with my forehead pressing on the ground as well. Then an explosion, and my spinal cord was erupting in flames, and my hair was quickly catching on fire.

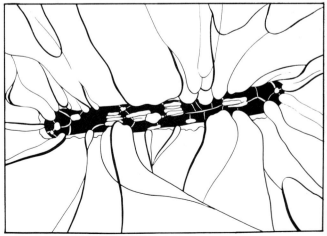

Cartoons: Fire.

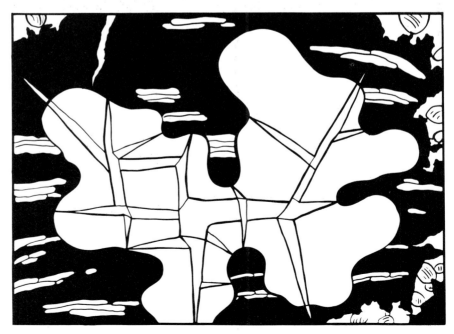

African Images

Some images evoke a sense of timelessness, whether they were made ten or two thousand years ago. This quality I feel in some African masks. They stir up a latent genetic memory of a tribal past, they awaken an awareness and a vague nostalgia difficult to define with words.

These modest images for glass are drawn from African masks and sculptures because I wanted to pay homage to them, and also because I wanted to suggest that the use of ethnic themes by all of you will bring fresh and powerful images into a medium almost worn thin and bloodless by our Western tradition. I responded to their alive presence.

Dream: I got out of bed one morning and went to the bathroom to shave. I looked in the mirror; instead of my face, an ancient dusty mask, made out of wood and straw, looked at me. At my shock, it laughed!

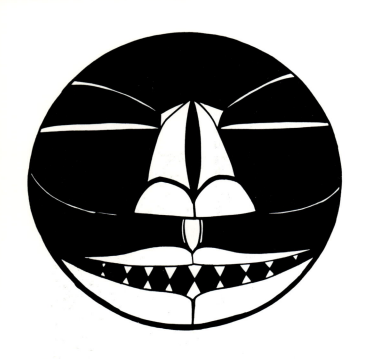

Cartoons from African wood carvings and masks.

A Look at the Way Glass Shatters

The way glass shatters under stress or when hit by a blunt object is very interesting. When glass cracks it forms a series of very powerful lines. Don't fail to see the beautiful designs that broken glass forms. Without exception those cracks reveal the nature of the material. In a strange way, a shattered window carries in it the frozen memory of a violent moment, a tantrum, a rifle shot, a thrown rock.

If you shatter a window and then reconstruct it by glazing it together again, you will redirect once again that original energy and recycle it into a completely different dimension.

Think of using shatter lines in your work. They add tension and interest. Look at the interesting effect. How beautiful are the hundreds of chance lines that crisscross the old cathedral windows. The windows were constructed with harmony of line and composition. Then time added a powerful commentary of its own, reminding you of the mortality of the work, and of the nature of the material.

Dream: My face was made of clear glass. As I was growing older, I could feel it cracking, all the breaks originating from my eyes. I remember also the image of a red rose through the clear and frost-covered glass of my broken skin.

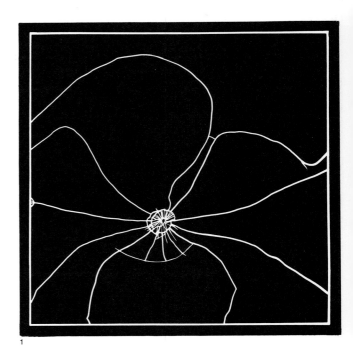

1

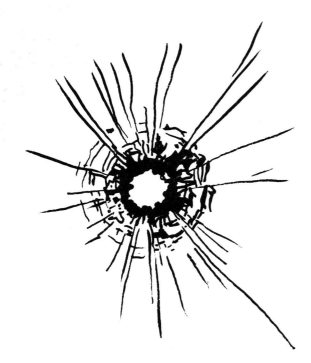

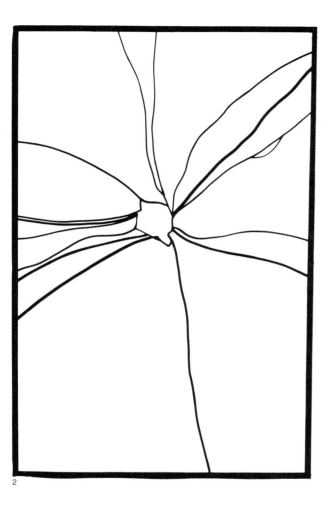

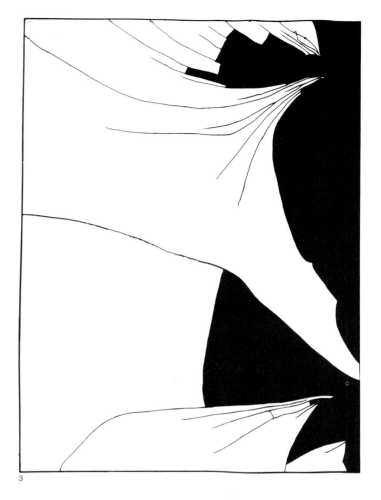

1. Shattered mirror.
2. Shattered panel of glass.
3. Shattered window still in its frame.

3

Introduction

Consider a cable, a thick complicated cable, and then cut it across with a clean blow. Simultaneously you will see all of the strands that concurrently but independently move through it. The different colors of the plastic casings will identify the different electrical currents, each one coming from a different source and going to a different place.

This chapter is a cross section of the themes that excite and trouble my life and concurrently but independently run through it.

I find it absolutely crucial to express what makes me feel alive here, today, in any possible way. Even before I am an artist, be it painter, maker of glass windows, mime, or teacher, I feel, I smell, I dream, I am excited or terribly sad, I see, and I am moved. Then for some mysterious reason I wish to vibrate, to move, to alter, to express, to transform.

The danger of any medium, of any art-form, is the role it gives us when we practice it for a long time. I feel it defines us too narrowly. Suddenly I am a stained glass maker, a specialized person; the discipline boxes me in. For this reason, I feel it is crucial for me to keep my vision fresh, to question why I do the things I do, to rediscover constantly the medium I use rather than be comfortable in it, and avoid feeling too secure in what I already know.

Ultimately, the most honest thing is to say "I don't know who I am." I must have the courage to keep it that way and not yield to the insecurity that follows and the subsequent desire to define myself completely. I must constantly go back to myself and even further back to that area of "unformed chaos" inside of which all of the diverse activities are truly meshed and one, and emerge time and time again a different person. If I can do this, my work will live, be it a window, a painting, a dance. To me, working is simultaneous with going further and further back to the source, the "pure potential," where anything is possible, alive, always present, and forever a surprise—funny, sad, tragic, grotesque, but never predictable.

Yet to liberate this potential, I feel I must demand of myself an effort that seems to be in the contrary direction. Nothing is worse than being clumsy with one's own tools, not knowing the materials one uses and not being completely familiar with the techniques for their use. Without a complete grasp of these, "poetic liberation" is impossible. So I explore my medium as much as possible (and this exploration is so time-consuming!), being careful not to get caught by all the preconceptions and terrible habits—mental and physical—that come with the prolonged use of a material.

I have been a painter for many years, and my involvement with stained glass began in response to my observation that glass as a material (because of its connection with light) seemed to have the capacity to move the viewer more than paint did. I began working in glass with the vague desire to have a deeper connection with an audience, and later I saw the potential and the excitement of seeing my work as an intrinsic part of an environment rather than merely an addition, tacked on after its completion. To me, becoming involved in stained glass has meant a personal growth in many directions. I have had to come out from being immersed only in my inner world to deal with the excitement, as well as the letdowns, of trying to articulate my ideas into specific environments and for a very specific group of people. Suddenly the audience has a real presence and a real face.

Glass held together by lead has struck me as being a material of unequaled beauty because of the myriad ways it transmits light and its subtle and varying shades of transparency and opacity. Glass has a magic to it that is perfect for expressing those inner psychological states that interest me, as in "My Androgynous Shadow," "Stained Glass Suicide," and "Eva," all independent panels of my figure series. The inner perception of androgyny, the desire for

a violent self-destruction, and an image of fertility are the motivating themes of these works, but to me a window is not fully realized if it does not reveal something about the physical properties of the material of which it is made. In such a way, "My Androgynous Shadow" and "Stained Glass Suicide" are also a commentary on the brittleness of glass, on the way it cracks because of expansion or direct impact by bullets, while "Eva" or my "Reflection" windows attempt to reveal the liquidity of glass, one of its most beautiful characteristics.

Confronting myself, my life in its totality, I have found my posture as an artist isolated and ineffectual. I find that one's own inner perception of the richness of life is only the beginning of a meaningful contribution. With stained glass I see

the potential to give much pleasure, much joy. To be able to make such a contribution to the life of others makes me feel good, so I have begun using this medium as a way out of my own feeling of alienation.

For this reason I have become very interested in the use of stained glass not only for the construction of single independent panels, but merged meaningfully with contemporary architecture where it can be experienced by many people. The medium because of its beauty almost naturally suggests its usefulness. In today's society the creation of really beautiful, meaningful environments is very very important.

As I am coming out of a shell of Self-perception and am connecting with society, I am confronted with a reality complex and full of problems, tensions, possibilities; consciously or unconsciously, I must decide what role I will take in the scheme of things.

To me, to exist and to be sensitive is simultaneously a totally political and a poetic act.

The Themes

I have done windows or designs for stained glass on each of the following subjects, and this text is an introduction, a way of explaining in a few words, why these motifs are interesting to me and in themselves. This chapter represents a thematic reality that is not static but ever-changing. With time, I will make more windows on the Narcissus theme and on the theme of meditation, complete the works in progress on the birth windows, and complete in glass my six-paneled screen design with dancers.

The works shown are understandably diverse in style since some (the Narcissus series) were done in 1970, and the latest ones (the figures from the magic theatre and dance section) were done in early 1975.

The themes are varied and diverse. I claim to be no scholar nor am I an expert on the subjects; rather I am a maker of images who wishes to introduce his own work in light of existing literature and references.

In my life I have come close to these motifs not by choice, but by finding myself entangled in their midst, and then realizing it. My understanding of these subjects, then, does not come from profound intellectual clarity but rather from "feel" and intuition.

Each one of us has a life story. Each story has its myth and its neurosis. As it unfolds, this story makes visible the few crucial issues it revolves around, and the passing of time gives us more prospective as to the meaning of those issues. In this respect each of the windows and designs is not an illustration of an abstract idea I chose, but has its roots and beginnings in my life experience—in all of its every-day quality.

Whether nothing happens by chance or everything happens by chance does not matter; signs emerge all around in the circumstances of our every-day life and in our very patterns of thought and perception that express a potential to flower or to rot. To attempt to control the meaning and the shape of our life is hopeless, but to be sensitive to it and express it clearly—whether it be bleak or luminous—is very possible.

Signs, clues, omens come in the oddest ways, and are always a surprise, mixed in with melodrama or even humor at times. For me, the interest in the Narcissus myth dates from a long time past, but came into focus by way of a personal circumstance—the poignant accusation of a person close to me that I was totally locked within myself and my art (it being my own reflection), and the cutting observation that I was unaware of the reality outside of myself as having a life of its own.

So you find a strand, whatever it may be, make no judgment on it, and begin pulling and tugging on it slowly until the whole carpet comes undone. Soon you will be much beyond the area of a personal problem. To begin following a theme is like walking in a forest you have never entered before; new animals, plants and places appear, some in the sun and some in the shade.

Is freedom then a sense of going with the grain of the wood? A harmony with Nature? An acceptance of its laws, its impersonal immensity moving through time, unstoppable, expressing itself through everything including our instinctive drives—sexual, then procreational and parental—and then resignation to our disappearance? Or is freedom in the flowering of our individual sensitivity, beauty, feelings, to the limit of contrivance (much like the act of a mime). Is freedom the futile attempt to escape out of time, out of life, in whatever way we think possible? Does this course lead to inevitable suicide?

I know I have no answers. I hope to have enough strength at least to ask the questions.

Is to love my life sane or suicidal? How can I deny all along some hidden desire not to exist? Having been close to dear friends who chose to end life while still young raises feelings and questions that trouble me and leave me with no resolution. For me the beginning of the practice of meditation started with the clear feeling that I could no longer trust my very perceptions and thoughts. My whole system began to feel beside the point, inadequate for its task of understanding. Confused and enough at the end of the rope I saw no other escape, but underneath, toward the center. To sit down and meditate was to face my chronic restlessness head-on.

So one seeks a new way to seek oneself, with new tools like silence, stillness, breath. You remain inescapably what you are, at the same time free and bound, in a soundless space.

I see myself only as a reflection on water, at times clear and sharp, at other times wobbling and distorting on its surface. Most peculiar is the perception that I am reflecting nothing, no person is on the pool's edge to reflect, substantial, real.

But if the figure of Narcissus—the mythical figure—evokes a reality static in character, in precarious balance between the danger of vanity and authentic connectedness to the core of reality, his close companion, Orpheus, is so much in motion, so alive!

His stance is clear, unquestionably an affirmation of joy articulated through song. Harmony rules over random and impersonal violence, harmony is the glue that makes life not only tolerable but so profoundly precious.

Song and music enchant, express, evoke; they do not merely describe. The waves of music create the inescapable need to move, to dance, to be, as naturally as boats sway and are responsive to the water that supports and moves them.

The body becomes itself through motion, and can go even further. It becomes a mask, takes on more and more identities. It can inhabit and make visible all those shadowy presences we feel inside ourselves but dare not express in our daylight existence. It becomes a vibrating antenna anywhere——in a dance hall, on a stage, or on a hilltop in the Sonora Desert gesturing unintelligible movements in the wind, waiting.

Breath

Moment after moment, everyone comes out from nothingness. This is the true joy of life.
—Shunryu Suzuki,
Zen Mind, Beginner's Mind

From 1966 to 1970 I had the great fortune to meet and study with two extraordinary Zen masters, Suzuki Roshi and Katagiri Roshi. Having had the opportunity to meditate with them and to experience their strength and wisdom changed the course of my life.

I remember very vividly that period when Suzuki Roshi was alive and Katagiri Roshi was in California. If I were to identify after many years what their major contribution to my life had been, I would mention first and be most grateful for the instruction in meditation I received from them, as well as the subsequent guidance in its meaning and practice.

They came from Japan and taught meditation to many of us in the West. By doing so, they have given us a new tool to work with in our perception of ourselves and of reality. They have put in the realm of direct experience a "form" perfected by many masters in the East for centuries, and made it relevant to us.

One of the newer aspects of this way for us is the concept that progress in understanding cannot happen without the full participation of the body, linking inseparably the intellectual process and the physical body into one "practice," one effort of transformation.

At the foundation of this practice lies breath. The experience of our breath is the "hum" of being alive. Exhales and inhales, a prolonged experience of our breath, will slowly still our mind, will force us to question our very own thought and who we are, and will slowly turn our attention to our center.

I made these stained glass windows out of gratitude to and in honor of these two Zen masters. "Blue Buddha Hand" is in the main hall at the Zen Center, 300 Page Street, San Francisco, while "The Rice Bowl" is in the library of the Soto Zen Monastery, Tassajara Hot Springs, in the mountains east of Big Sur, California.

1

2

1,2. *Blue Buddha Hand,* 1971, 27″×41″, San Francisco
   Zen Center: The window and detail. (See p. 25.)

1

1–3. *The Rice Bowl,* 1971, 32″×44″, Soto Zen Monastery, Tassajara Hot Springs, California: The window, two details. (See p. 25.)

2

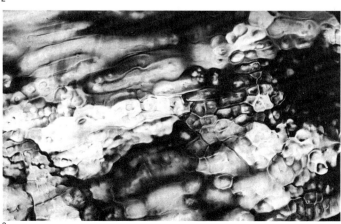

3

Narcissus: A Self-Portrait

Iste ego sum! sensi; nec mea fallit imago;/uror amore mei, flammas moveoque feroque/quid faciam? roger, anne rogem? quid deinde rogabo? quod cupio, mecum est: inopem me copia fecit.

Oh I am he! I have felt it, I know now my own image. I burn of love of my own self; I both kindle the flames and suffer them. What shall I do, shall I woo or be wooed? Why woo at all? What I desire I have, the very abundance of my riches beggars me.
—Ovid

E ne l'incendio d'una fredda stampa mentre il viso so bagna, il petto au-ampa.

And while his face is bathing his bosom is kindled with the fire of a cold picture.
—Marino

Narcissus is the beautiful young boy who in the Greek myth rejected the love of others, and fell in love with his own image. Looking at himself in the water he withered away and died. After his death his body was transformed into a beautiful flower.

Narcissus is not a hero figure; he is young and tender in age. His appearance is beautifully in balance between the masculine and the feminine. He rejects the living experiences that make life a continuous cyclical change from adolescence to old age.

He seeks himself instead. Fixed in contemplation of his own beauty, he loves himself. He wishes that he were enough, and that no difference existed between the masculine and the feminine, the lover and the loved, time past and time present, the world of reality and that of reflection.

I made the Narcissus series for a house in northern California. The first three windows—"Birth," "Transformation," and "Death"—were built together in the summer of 1970; the last one, "The Tantrum," was an added afterthought on the theme, executed in the summer of 1971. It portrays the perfect resolution of the Narcissus situation as a mirror in the shape of the flower, and the lack of resolution of that situation by the shatter marks running through the clear and mirrored surface, as if a rock had been thrown through it in frustration.

1

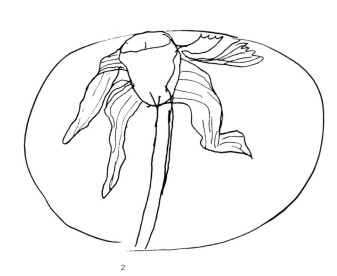

2

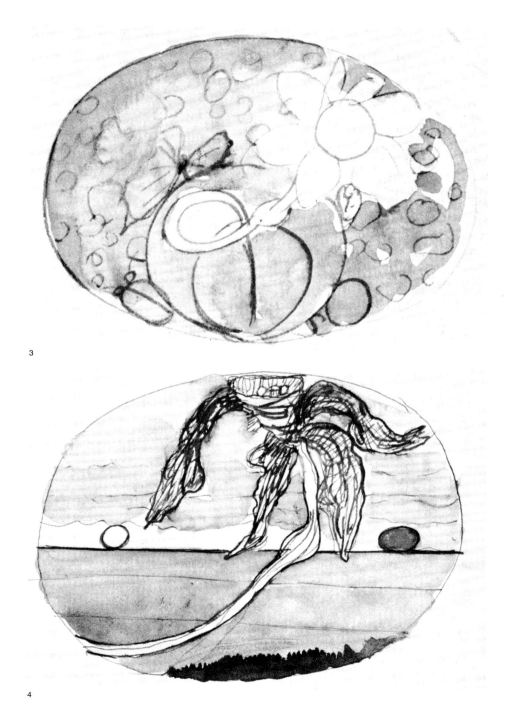

3

4

1–8. Preliminary sketches for Narcissus series.

5

6

7

8

9

9. Exterior view of *Birth*, Narcissus series.

10

10. *Birth*, Narcissus series, 1970, 34″ × 46″. (See p. 24.)
11. *Transformation*, Narcissus series, 1970, 34″ × 46″. (See p. 24.)

12

13

12. *Death,* Narcissus series, 1970, 34″ × 46″. (See p. 24.)
13. *The Tantrum,* Narcissus series, 1971, 34″ × 46″. (See p. 24.)

Music and Birth

Drängender Zweig an Zweig,
nirgends ein freier . . .
Einer! o steig . . . o steig . . .
Aber sie brechen noch.
Dieser erst oben doch
biegt sich zur Leier.

Branch crowding on branch
not one of them free . . .
One! o climb . . . o climb . . .
But still they break.
Yet this top one at last
bends into a lyre.
—Rainer Maria Rilke,
"Sonnets to Orpheus,"
translated by M. D. Herter Norton

Long hours of pushing an ice pack on her back, breathing with her and being weakened and ripped apart by watching her go through the fierce pain of labor. Suddenly the tip of the head becomes clearly visible. Suddenly a change of mood. The head is visible and it stays there, sunken in wet veils of flesh, pushing them apart, keeping them taut.

For hours we both felt shaken and in motion, as though running, chased by a relentless wind. Then at the appearance of his head, the wind stops and there is a sudden quiet. You look at the tip of this little guy and he is there, waiting to be born, completely held and contained in this human vessel. For a moment, before its beginning, you can see his life in its entirety. You see him go through so many experiences, discoveries and transformations . . . oh, all those emotions! . . . and then disappear, and you see all the space and silence after that. Then a sudden gust of wind of the "on and on"—a sudden contraction bears on the little one and it bursts him outside on his own.

You can hear the clock ticking, the nurses talking; the doctor focuses on the newborn. He cleans him and feels the cord to make sure all the blood has flowed into him, then he cuts him loose. The doors open again to the world of chatter and fleeting emotions. I am tired and I want to sleep.

With its richness of colors ranging from crimson to purples to grays, with its glossy surfaces, with its animal presence of blood, cord, and placenta, with bones and flesh coming out of bones and flesh, with continuous flow of fleeting expressions and emotions to light itself and the whisper of time, is birth not made for glass?

The drawings of birth windows show works in progress. The guitar shape betrays my weakness for music.

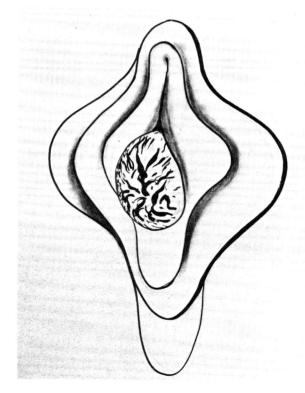

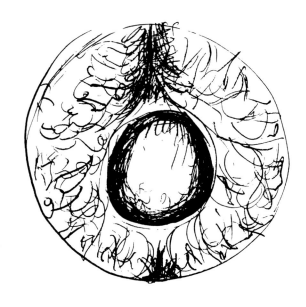

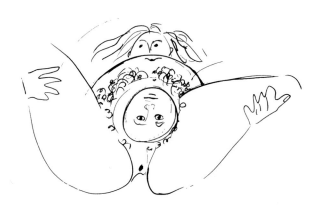

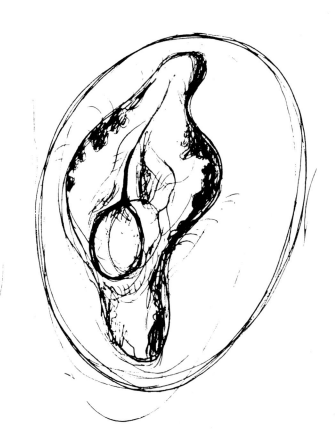

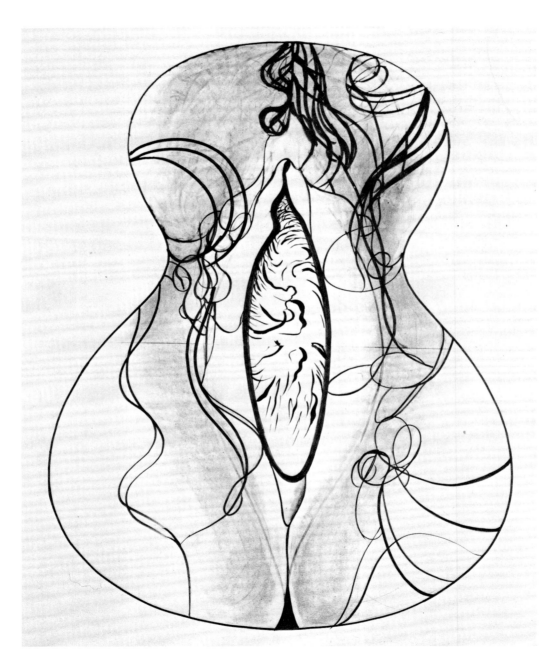

Cartoon: *Becoming Visible*, 1973.

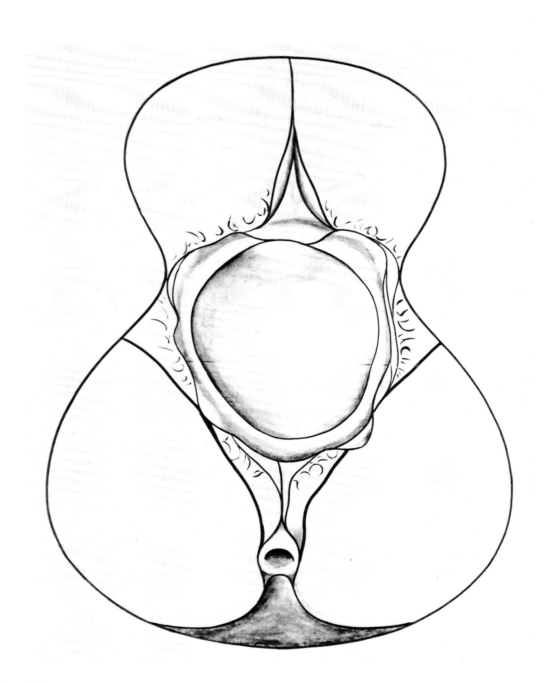

Cartoon: *Being Born,* 1973.

Carlos Castaneda's Don Juan

The moths carry a dust on their wings, he said, a gold dust, that dust is the dust of knowledge.
—Don Juan

Like many others, I have read the recently published and popular books of Carlos Castaneda. Like many others, I was amazed, moved and confused. For those who have not read the books, all four recount the relationship and apprenticeship of Carlos Castaneda, a young anthropologist, to Don Juan, a Yaqui Indian and a man of knowledge. Castaneda recounts chronologically his visits with Don Juan, and reports with vivid clarity his experiences in the Sonora Desert.

Central to the theme in these books is Don Juan's contention that most of us don't experience reality in its mysterious and awesome fullness, but rather that we block it out. Our senses experience a "description" of the world, one we learned. That description is inaccurate, safe, and more like a screen blocking an infinite space.

Through the association of these two men, we follow Carlos as he is progressively entering a "painful crisis." His most basic, instinctual and neurological sense of life (not to speak of his rational mind) is shattered and continuously challenged by Don Juan.

By being incessantly confronted with "impossible occurrences," Carlos senses that the foundation of his very own relationship to reality is crumbling. Simultaneously, he enters and participates in a world of luminous beings, strange sounds and presences.

In this realm, inexplicable transformations occur, revealing a world terrifying, fantastic, and also very humorous. What reaches me in these books are the rich images and moods and incredible situations. We walk and feel the desert's chaparral and the mysterious spaces it contains; we feel the winds and currents that traverse it.

I have no answer to the questions these books pose to me as a reader attempting to understand them logically; intuition can evaluate the value of the material much better. As a maker of windows I respond to the wealth of source material and even more to its magic mood. Stained glass is such a perfect medium to express just such mind and space dimensions.

The cartoons are not literal renditions of any specific moments or events in these books, but an attempt to translate into glass design the feel of these pages.

The model for the figure of Don Juan is a very loved friend who has been in my life the door to the unknown—the friend who will take me away, crying and laughing, while sipping English tea with milk and sugar.

Studies for *Neil as Don Juan.*

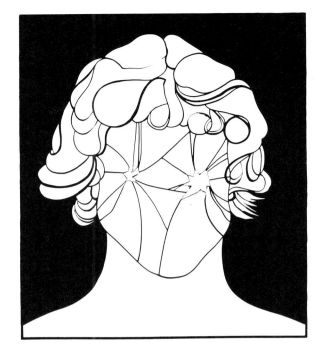
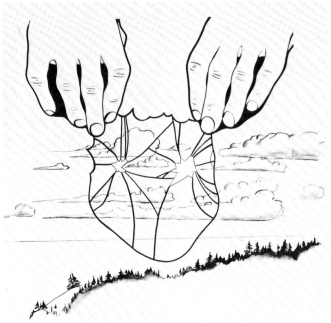
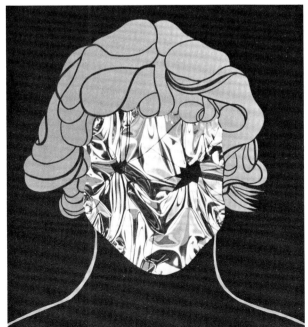

The Magic Theatre of Shadows

What is a shadow? Your unsubstantial self walking around with you, mimicking every one of your movements to perfection, graphically making fun of you by distorting your shape on walls, on the ground. Your shadow crawls in front of you or behind you or to your side. It shows how grotesque and beautiful you are, but also it reveals your exact relationship to the sun.

This shadow presence is an intimate, essential, and theatrical commentary on your being where you are. Use it if you can. It is so expressive!

Have a bottle of wine at hand, and clear the walls of a room. Then darken it and have only one source of light, one you can move about. Then with your lover, your son, your friend, or all of them, dance, carry on, and play with your shadows. Music, good humor and wine will make you appreciate the lively shapes on the wall. They're but a step away from where you are and so vividly express the character of the people they reflect.

Then, if you can stand still, when your shadow appears to be particularly beautiful or funny, "freeze"—and have your lover trace your silhouette, and you trace your lover's.

Not the traditional way to begin a cartoon, but it is a way! The next day, with calm and a cold "eye," look at those silhouettes. Choose some particularly expressive ones and begin there. Fill them, if you want, inside and out with images.

Among the seemingly difficult barriers not so easily broken in the making of stained glass is that of "motion" and, even more so, that of "spontaneity." These barriers are difficult because of the time element involved in construction of a window, and the nature of the technique itself. To me this seemingly bizarre way to begin a cartoon is only one of the ways to achieve more freshness and directness in the image.

The cartoons and windows in this section, as well as in the next two, attempt to bring back a new regard for the figure, which has, in the past few decades, been stylized, abused or altogether ignored—with the exception of Jeffrey Speeth, whose work is represented in Chapter 5.

1. Preliminary study: *Neil* (negative print), 1974.
2. Preliminary study: *To Burn in the Wind*, 1975.

1

2

3

4

5

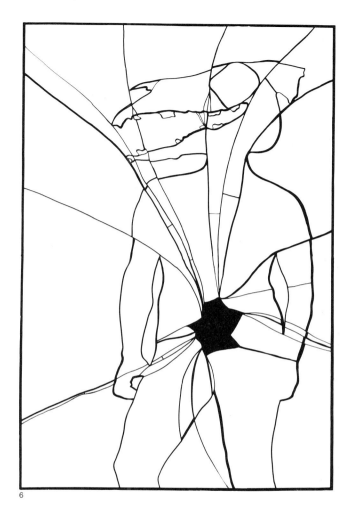

6

3. *Eva,* 1975, 46″ × 72″. (See p. 26.)
4. Cartoon: *The Embrace,* 1974.
5. Cartoon: *Wandering Restlessly,* 1974.
6. Cartoon: *Dream of the Horse's Skull,* 1974.

7

8

9

10

7. Cartoon: *Death in My Heart*, 1974.
8. The window: *My Androgynous Shadow*.
   (See p. 26.)
9. The author and his shadow in black glass.
10. The shadow cast by *My Androgynous Shadow*.

Suicide

Any careful considerations of life entails reflection on death, and the confrontation with reality means facing mortality. We never come fully to grips with life until we are willing to wrestle with death. We need not speculate about death and its place in the scheme of things to make a simple point; every deep concern, whether with oneself or with another, has in it the problem of death. And the problem of death is posed most vividly in suicide. Nowhere is death so near.
—James Hillman
Suicide and the Soul

I have felt life discolor, I have been unresponsive to any sensation; I have sensed my whole body go flat, become stale. Occasionally I indulge in this void and wish to vanish, to "not exist," to leap over.

The works of mine presented in this section come from the part of me that feels forever about to drown. They are an attempt at working my way out of the absurdity of being alive but not feeling that I am. They are a confrontation with these very feelings, and a meditation on the unresolved and disquieting corners of my experience.

I have wondered if glass with its inherent connection with light tends toward the beautiful, or does it seem so only because we have chosen to use it primarily to express joy? I wonder if the medium has a message of its own, or can we effectively bend light against itself to express any content whatsoever, even the most negative and hopeless?

Following are a stained glass window, a painting and a cartoon, printed in the negative, on the theme of suicide.

1. The window: *Stained Glass Suicide.* (See p. 27.

2

3

2. Detail: Right hand while window on easel.
3. Detail: Right arm and hand in completed window.

4

4. Window in process: Detail of shattered mirror.
5. Detail from completed window.
6. Detail: Hole sandblasted into glass.

5

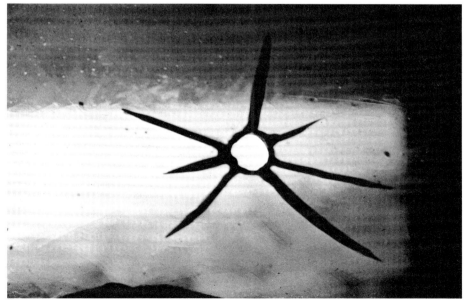

6

7. Cartoon: *Suicide,* negative print.
8. Oil painting on canvas: *Gun Nozzle Mandala,*
   1973, 6-foot diameter.

8

Dance

*You think it horrible that lust and
rage should dance attention upon my
old age;
they were not such a plague when I
was young;
what else have I to spur me into song?*
—W. B. Yeats

Dance itself certainly needs no introduction! Some of its qualities especially fascinate me, however, and are worth mentioning. In dance we attempt to re-experience our "archetypal self," to re-capture a fluid and unencumbered, possibly mythic, image of what we feel we are. Most interesting is that dance can be an abandonment to "chaos" and at the same time an emergence from it—loss of control and discovery of form.

A beautiful dance seems to be so much more than the addition of movements in sequence.

The figures in this watercolor design for a six-paneled stained glass screen now in "progress, are executed with the same shadow technique I outlined in the Magic Theatre section. They are not the shadows of professional dancers but those of friends I met while dancing and enjoying myself, at night, in San Francisco bars and night clubs, dreaming behind my painted face in the glitter and the red lights.

This installation of glass, light, and lead I made especially for the show "Works in Glass," held in November, 1975, at the Emanuel Walter Gallery of the San Francisco Art Institute. In this conceptual piece, I sought to break down the components of glass work and isolate them. Two dancers, made of mirror, lie on the floor while their distorted image is reflected with light on the wall. On an adjoining wall, I executed a drawing in lead only, outlining two shadow silhouettes of the same dancer.

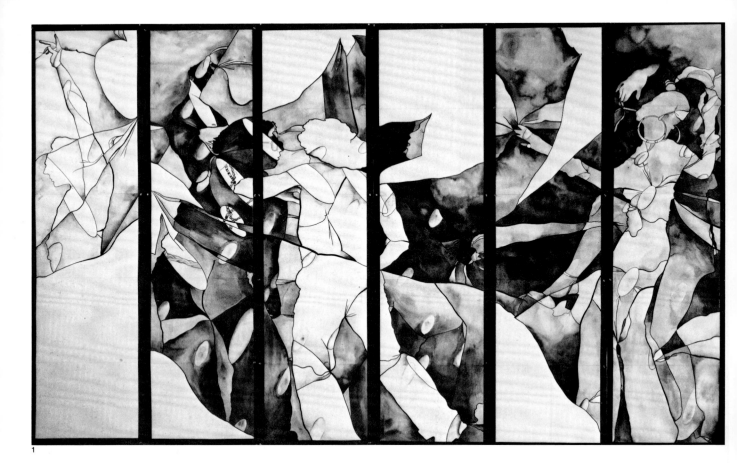

1

1. Watercolor design for six-paneled stained glass
   screen, *Dancing, Dancing, Dancing . . . San
   Francisco Cabaret, 1972-1975,* 1975, 7′ × 12′.
   (See p. 28.)
2. Light, glass, and lead installation, San Francisco Art Institute, 1975, Left: *Dancing, Dancing . . . and Flying Away,* a piece in mirror and
   light. Right: *Varna,* a drawing in lead.

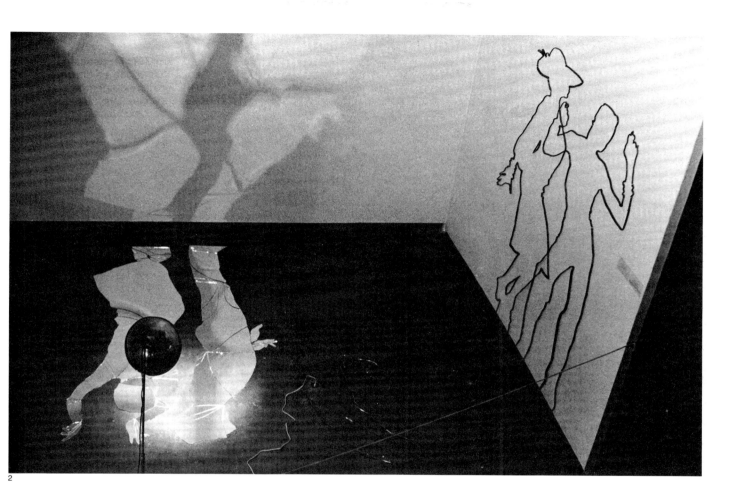

2

4

Designing Environments

A beautifully made, spacious, stained glass environment is truly a joy to be in. With the sensitive control of light and forms, it can envelop us in a magic veil. Unlike a specific art object which we can experience and then leave, a full environment is always with us or, better, we are included in it. It contains us in a maternal way; its quality tints our experience throughout the day and expresses the day itself.

A beautiful environment, whatever its shape or character, stands as living proof of a successful collaboration of all the people who put it together.

A large project is always much more than the idea of one individual. The architect, the artist, the person or group who commissioned it, the craftmen who did much of the work, and the public as the users are all part of one event, equal participants in its creation and subsequent meaning.

In this book so far I have looked at stained glass itself, trying to reveal some of its intrinsic potential as a medium. I have also pointed out how source material, interesting in itself and also as an observation on personal experience, can be expressed and can flower through the use of glass, light and lead.

Everything I have written and illustrated so far is scaled to what an individual as a unit can create with his own hands. The windows and designs shown so far can be executed by one person. If we now take the logical step of wanting to create or appreciate windows that extend themselves much beyond being small apertures of light to the outside, but become an enveloping presence, we find ourselves dealing with a whole new set of problems and considerations.

Picture yourself working in a room or studio, filled with your photographs, your oils, your glass, or whatever materials you use. The objects of your creation are pulling you, affecting you, as well as puzzling you. You are constantly struggling with the meaning of what you are doing. You ask yourself, "Why am I doing this?" But you are overrun by the necessity to express what you have in mind and, with or without an answer, you continue to work. Perhaps you seek the meaning through the very working.

Then picture someone else, effected, moved or perplexed by the experience of your work in the gallery or in your studio. A critic tries to evaluate the meaning of your work—its logic, its poetic or intellectual value—but whatever the opinions, the work is always related to itself, as though you are establishing the meter by which you will be judged at the same time you work.

Finally, picture yourself designing an entire environment for yourself and someone else. Suddenly, in the process, you will have to deal with many problems much beyond your own intrinsic interests and inner poetic tensions.

The spaces we live in and the way we use them express who we are in a total way. If we wander in the old hallways of a stone-built medieval monastery, the very stones speak of the minds, customs and deep-felt feelings of the monks of the time. Let's follow a monk into his barren cell. To him, that cell is beautiful—a perfect place to fulfill his destiny undistracted by superfluous objects. Yet to a contemporary and frivolous dandy, that same cell lacks meaning because it is devoid of the necessary sensuosity which is the very object and reassurance of the worth of his existence.

If we stay in an old Parisian hotel, the spaces, the wallpaper, the woodwork, nearly everything in the room, expresses a flavor, a sense of life with its own style, customs, values. If we are capable then of translating "what we see" into "what it is" and "what it means," we can be anywhere—in Reno, Nevada, or in a farmhouse in Tennessee. We can make the connection anywhere: that any object finds its own definition not only because of what it is in itself, but for the way in which it is used. "The meaning is the use," says Wittgenstein, the Viennese philosopher.

When the implications of this idea are fully absorbed, the designer or artist blossoms into a mature being, dealing at the same time with all the inner tensions that an ongoing dialogue with himself will produce. Without losing his hold on his own center, he comes to grips with all outer problems and issues of his work in the larger social context.

Becoming a designer of environments, then, involves dealing with much more than merely the aesthetic or functional issues; it means facing why we live as we live, and understanding clearly what it is that the things and images around us express.

I have come to feel that wherever a vague desire for growth and change begins, the mere reworking of the aesthetics of an environment is not sufficient, but is a superficial approach to the resolution of change that glosses over the real issues. Without an examination of our beliefs, of our life style that is in turn rooted in a particular economic reality, no outer change in the space arrangements or light arrangements will effect life's meaning, but will become merely an entertaining event.

I have come to witness in our culture a compulsive desire to create something new for its own sake, and I have felt a subsequent nausea at observing the indulgence of this effort to refresh people's environments and lives by

Three Attitudes toward Design

mere manipulation of the outer world. Only a radical transformation at our very core has any meaning at all, and this requires an effort to reexamine what work is and how we spend our time and why. The creation of newer environments will happen by itself.

Try as an exercise giving a cold distant look at the place in which you live. There, observe hour by hour for a full day your actions, your thoughts and emotions. Slowly your observation will yield a picture of you not felt from the inside but experienced from the outside. Time and space co-penetrate each other and their meeting point is the environments in which we live.

Making an environment, then, can be an act of liberation, an effort to untangle ourselves from the binding restrictions of our individual neurosis or from the neurosis of our social class; on the other hand it could be an act of collaboration, a reaffirming and blossoming of the existing social values and mores, as well as repressions.

Emilio Ambastz, in his introduction to *Italy, The New Domestic Landscape: Achievements and Problems of Italian Design,* a catalogue published by the Museum of Modern Art for their exhibition, ascribes three basic attitudes to the diverse work of contemporary Italian design. These attitudes are relevant today to any person producing anything at all.

"It is possible to differentiate [in Italy] today three prevalent attitudes toward design: the first is conformist, the second is reformist, and the third is rather one of contestation, attempting both inquiry and action.

"By the first, or conformist, approach we refer to the attitude of certain designers who conceive of their work as an autonomous activity responsible only to itself; they do not question the sociocultural context of their work, but instead continue to refine already established forms and functions. . . .

"Their work (which constitutes the most visible part of Italian design production) is mainly concerned with exploring the aesthetic quality of single objects. . . .

"The second, or reformist attitude, is motivated by a profound concern for the designer's role in a society that fosters consumption as one means of inducing individual happiness, therefore insuring social stability. Torn by the dilemma of having been trained as creators of objects, and yet being incapable of controlling either the significance or the ultimate uses of their objects, they find themselves unable to reconcile the conflicts between their social concerns and their professional practices. . . .

The End of an Age

"In their ambiguous attitude toward the object, these designers justify their activity by giving to their designs shapes that deliberately attempt a commentary upon the roles that these objects are normally expected to play in our society.

"The third approach to design which we have designated as one of contestation, reveals itself in two main trends in Italy today, each trying to get at the root in very different ways, the first by a commitment to a "moratorium position" and an absolute refusal to take part in the present socioindustrial system. Here "antiobject" means "not making objects" and the designer's pursuits are either confined to political action and philosophical postulation, or else consist of total withdrawal."

As a painter and maker of glass veils, I participate and operate in a culture with its character and values. The possible relationships between an individual artist and this time and this society are many, and each type of contact has its own type of pleasure and pain.

Personally I feel I was trained to respect and value primarily my sensitivity and individual identity. The tradition of painting in the West in the last hundred years itself suggests that a meaningful art work comes out of the will and intuition of a single individual. I ask myself seriously if the "creative individual" as commonly understood is not a residue from the past, an obsolete creature.

In the past hundred years, artists have developed a sense of their work as something valid in itself—it seems to me these years were the time for the strong ego. Today I wonder if the flowering of culture and creative growth must happen without the deification of the individual ego. The path of the individual artist sensitive only to his own inner world has lost its vitality and is a sterile one. The potential for ego-gratification so possible in the past has become a hollow experience for the artist and is replaced by a vague sense of anxiety and discomfort, since society, faced with the immense problems of a changing age, does not really know how to integrate either the artist's work or his expectations in any meaningful way.

Within myself, I feel the divergent pull of two seemingly completely different desires. The one is asocial, to live out my individual destiny regardless of anything else, a lyrical path, clearly pointing to the enjoyment of decadence. The other pull is social, to find the meaning of my very existence through the ability to "relate," judging the worth and success of my work not only by its intrinsic quality or flavor, but by its capacity to be integrated into a much larger fabric.

Pleasure and Collective Experience

I feel strongly that the ability to communicate requires the courage to live, as well as to die, while being tuned in only to myself requires only the courage to die.

Since our culture has made for artists the concepts of creativity and individuality almost synonymous to each other in the past century, as a person I feel the pain and contradiction of this upbringing. Confronted with the experience of contemporary life, my desire is to dissolve and to be used anonymously as well as to realize myself as an individual. Ironically, desire for self-realization pushes me into wanting to be apart, and separated.

I feel this period to be the end of an age, and, the day's ending twilight is always a magnificent sight. The breaking down of values and mores, the loosening of the fibers of the fabric, allow the most insane and beautiful experiments in art and life. In our time, a very special, fascinating and unique freedom exists—not certainly the freedom of harmony and order, but of darkness, of excesses and chaos.

Returning to stained glass, let us remember again some of its characteristics. Whether it be used in small panels or in entire environments, the medium's intimate meshing with light make it a powerful and moving presence. It requires no education to be sensitive to light.

Our connection with light is so primal, so profound, that any sensitive and successful use of stained glass is bound to be of great pleasure to us. The perception of light is the perception of existence itself; it follows then that the construction of an environment dedicated to light itself becomes a celebration, a liberating experience.

Developing new images and new uses of the medium is a kind of parallel growth to the inventiveness of nature as it evolves. In the windows of Kathie Bunnell, for example, the subject is nature, yet the panels create a nature of their own, a profound, world complete with its own ecological balance.

Stained glass holds the potential for being used as the means for a "collective experience." A kind of human event can happen around its construction. Any large stained-glass work necessitates the energy of many people, each giving a unique contribution. Architect, designer, craftsman, public—all must interrelate and mingle with each other during the conception, execution and installation of the project. This mingling process is a very fertile time for the many people involved. At this time, vital information is exchanged between designer and architect, craftsmen or students and designer, the community who is going to receive the project, and the makers of it. This exchange alters everybody's consciousness in some way or other.

This process of collective participation points to a time when architects and designers may not exist separately from the community in which they live or build for as members of a separate social class, but when the people themselves, through the actual exercising of their creative ability by participation as groups or as individuals, will take possession of and shape their own spaces, establish their tastes and create their own indigenous culture according to necessity.

This idea might sound utopian if stated in such general terms as an abstract concept, but let's come closer to reality. Teachers in art programs everywhere can experiment, if they wish, with their students in the construction of large works that can be used by the communities in which they live.

At the beginning of such a program, the blueprint would have to be that of one or two artists and designers functioning as responsible directors for the whole process, with students working with them as apprentices. Later, as time passes, the studio may become a womb, a propitious and charged atmosphere for the birth of the ideas of any student who has experienced the

medium in depth and can take full responsibility for the process from design to installation. The studio will be at the same time a place to study and grow, and a place connected with the community around it as it produces work for that community's enjoyment.

Such a setup is not utopian at all; it is quite possible. It requires that artists who teach and members of art departments in colleges reexamine the purposes of their programs and the premises of their educational philosophies.

I am not implying that such a suggestion is a solution to the cultural contradiction of our time, but it may be a beginning. It strikes me as absurd that, on the one side, art schools graduate thousands of artists of whom only a minimal fraction will eventually make a living from their art, while, on the other side, hundreds of buildings—private and public—come into existence barren of any sensitive, interesting and integrated artwork.

Physical conditions can even be created so that windows may be built and installed not as permanent in a structure, but rather inserted temporarily in a pattern of openings. This setup would be appropriate for schools or other semipublic places. A wall of glass could then be a constantly changing event.

One of the highest peaks of art was realized in the great works of the collective, such as at Chartres, where the total cathedral itself is the expression of a whole culture. Notice that the contribution of any single individual is anonymous (how unlike us!) and flows in with the work of everyone else to help form the total statement. Such an experience is so unfamiliar in our industrial age when the relationship between individual and society is so unclear and jumbled that each artist has his or her own private language.

This aspect of the collective experience to which stained glass lends itself, and the potential for public use, has been of particular interest to me. So, during the summer of 1973, I conducted an experiment at the San Francisco Art Institute where I was teaching. I set out to find public places for which to construct large windows with the idea in mind that the students and I would build the panels in the classroom.

Robert Marquis, head of the architectural firm Marquis and Associates, was receptive and enthusiastic about the idea and provided us with two window placements in buildings his firm was designing.

The first window went into the hall of a senior citizens' apartment building. The other piece, in eight panels, was placed in a clearstory window of a child care center in the Hunter's Point area of San Francisco. The funds for the projects were raised from the city, as well as from the federal government.

Balancing between the architects, the communities for whom the windows were being made, the students, the art commission who had to approve of the designs, the college administration, the deadlines, and the contractors who finally installed the panels, was truly an experience!

The designs were my own in their embryonic form, and that was a pity. I had hoped students themselves would design the project, but we had only one full month for each commission—barely time enough to get the windows made —and the students were beginners.

Together we discussed the colors to be used, the lead design, and selected the glass. The students painted, fired and glazed the windows completely on their own. The experience was exciting for all of us involved, though not without its degree of misunderstandings and strain. Finally, when the windows were completed and installed, the useful by-product of this educational experiment is that two San Francisco communities have stained glass to enjoy as an integral part of buildings in which they will spend great parts of their lives.

In the photoessay that follows, photographer Susan Shaw captures some of the phases of the execution and installation of the piece at the senior citizens' apartment building.

The series of photographs, pages 146 through 159, show construction and installation of the window *Water Reflections*, a project at the college of the San Francisco Art Institute for the community.

146

Tracing the cartoon.

Cutting the glass.

Painting the glass.

Replacing the unwanted pieces.

Final touches.

Members of the San Francisco Art Commission
approve the project.

Soldering the window.

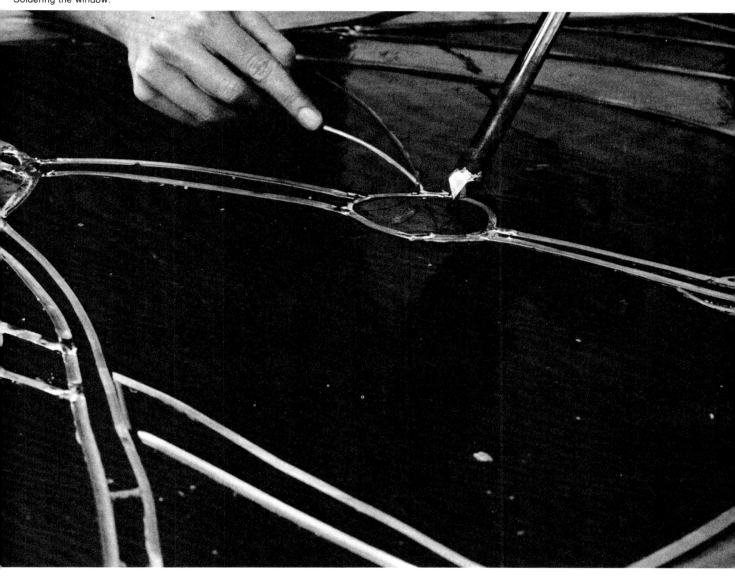

Soldering (below).
Making the reinforcing structure (right).

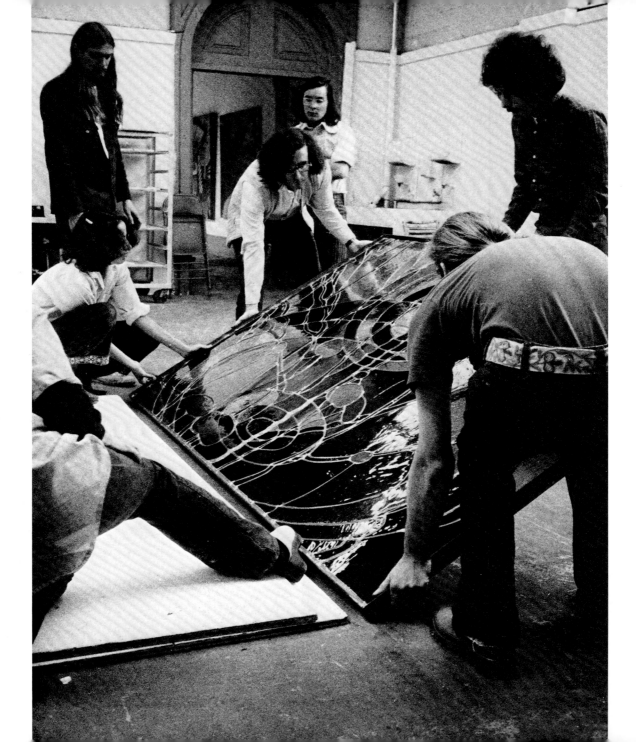

Raising the window for the first time (left).

Water Reflections, 1973, 5′ × 8′, finished and installed at the Senior Citizens Residence, 1750 McAllister, San Francisco (below).

The Making of Commissioned Work

The question of personal vision in commissioned work is seemingly a thorny one. A painter creating his work in his studio experiences a freedom as wide as his imagination and ability. For him the issue of his work's use comes only later. Many stained glass artists work in this fashion today, creating panels and dealing with the display of their work only after it is completed.

In a commissioned work, however, the problem of use is built into the design process itself, and to the maker of stained glass, it can cause quite a bit of strain, or great satisfaction.

Why do people make art objects at all? The *will* to create an image is ego rooted, but the *purpose* may be just the opposite. To want to express a thought by way of a work can be at the same time an act of release and an attempt to validate one's own ideas and vision. Seen in this light, art is an act of aggression. But the *content*, which I have called previously the purpose, is just the opposite of aggression. The content is what we share, enjoy, learn and gain insight from. It belongs to us all. In this respect the degree to which an artist is successful is the degree to which his presence fades away and his work becomes itself. The consciousness of an artist belongs to everybody; it is not his possession.

In commissioned work, the finished product must communicate. The creative work happens under much more pressure than does private work. To the artist, it is experienced as a very difficult balancing of his own inner necessities and insight with a sense of what is truly needed and appropriate to a specific physical environment, for the people who live in it.

Some artists find working under this pressure much too confining. A whole number of mishaps can happen in the process. Misunderstandings arise between architect and designer, or designer and client. A lack of adequate funds to execute the desired work might in turn force the designer to oversimplify the design and systematize the execution of the piece beyond the tolerable limit.

Be careful, then, if you plan large works. A successful environment is much more than the result of a good idea, but requires also the careful planning of all the steps that lead up to its execution and installation.

Working for an openminded, aware client can be very gratifying, because the whole process becomes much more personal. If the client is not open to the process, the client is a constant burden. He will want to impose his rather conventional ideas on the designer, while missing a dynamic vision and sense of what stained glass can do for him. If the client must know what he is going to get, where is the room for a true plunge into the unknown? Unless both designer and client have the capacity to take such a plunge, the work will be a mere replica of an already existing idea and, as such, will be stale. The client must trust the designer, and the designer the client, or nothing at all can happen!

When should the collaboration between architect and designer begin? The most obvious approach is that the architect designs the building, then calls the glass artist to work in specifically assigned apertures. This approach makes a lot of sense if the architect's understanding of light and stained glass is good.

Another form of collaboration creates an ongoing work relationship where the architect consults the glassmaker throughout the invention and design stages of his building, utilizing him as a special light expert. A good artist in stained glass is very aware of how glass-light can effect the mood and character of a space.

Both approaches are valid. I much prefer the second, since it forces and allows a much deeper relationship between the architecture and the stained glass.

For an artist designing architectural work, it is most important to understand what is most appropriate for any given situation. An intense emotional statement, for instance, is effective and appropriate only in the right context. Glasswork can range from a moving personal statement to a more impersonal and just as interesting presence.

The glass itself need not be blown, but could be industrially made, as well. I personally love the feel of those large sheets of Polaroid glass, or of that flawless shiny black. All of the industrially made sheets have the advantage of being available in large sizes.

Stained Glass for Houses

A stained glass panel may be commissioned for a home already lived in by the owner. He has an existing opening, and he likes your work. Such a situation is not uncommon. People have become so enthusiastic about a window they saw that they have knocked out an entire existing wall and redesigned the area around the newly acquired stained glass work. To know that such people are around warms my heart.

One may collaborate with an architect as he designs a house to plan the inclusion of glass into the house from conception. This route is very exciting, since once the architect and the artist do trust each other, their efforts can playfully accent and counterpoint each other's work.

Lightwells, skylights, and original space arrangements allow for a newer and less traditional use of the medium. However, when the amount of work consumed by a truly fine piece in stained glass is considered, the artist might feel upset at the realization that he is doing all that work for such a small audience.

Stained Glass for Public Buildings

Contemporary work in stained glass should definitely go into public buildings. The audience becomes so much larger and, since no one person must live all the time with the windows, the designer may make a much more forceful statement without it becoming an obsessive presence in anyone's private life.

I strongly encourage any artist in stained glass to attempt to add some light and joy in places we all use as much as we do our public buildings. I would love to lose myself into a beautifully vibrant blue stained glass window while waiting in line for my driver's license! Many problems and much red tape are involved in setting up such a situation; please don't give up trying!

Stained Glass in Churches

Entire books have been and could still be written about the vast field of stained glass in churches. The origins of stained glass art in the Middle Ages are so completely tied up with the support and use that the Gothic clergy gave to the new art. Today a vast number of people still associate the medium itself as something to be used only in churches, since they have not been exposed to any other noticeable use of it.

To understand this relationship between the church and stained glass, we must keep in mind the whole history of the church and its changing role in our culture as well as the history of stained glass as used in the churches and cathedrals, which reveals clearly the character of the church as it changed through time.

At the height of the Gothic age, the church urgently needed the newly discovered medium of stained glass. It expressed, with its magical presence, the passionate and mystical truths of the church. Glass was used with such feeling, and used to its fullest power! In that age the cathedral in any town in France or England was the heart of the community. Stained glass in that cathedral was intended to be a major means of speaking to the faithful. The windows and rose windows not only told the stories of the Old and New Testaments, but were much more. They shown like suspended multifaceted jewels of light, glowing in the dark interiors, perceptible proof of the ancient truths, overwhelming viewers into another dimension.

Today the established church is very different. It is no longer the central nervous system of the times, but is a peripheral force whose interests are much more tied up in the preservation of middle-class values. The church is conservative in character and avoids the very intensity and depth of experience that stained glass as a medium is capable of when used in a new and experimental way and to its fullest potential. In the United States, most church windows commissioned today from established stained glass studios reflect a repetition of old, lifeless patterns or are hopelessly modest in their use of contemporary forms and images. These windows don't represent any creative contribution to contemporary art.

The few groups of religious people who practice their beliefs with courage and depth are at the periphery of and are almost always at odds with the established and organized church authority. These groups do come to grips with the problems and issues of a changing time, but don't have the means, the energy, or the following to commission and undertake large works in stained glass, since they are so involved in their very survival.

Historical Look

Stained glass had barely come into existence when it reached an undisputed height in the thirteenth century, in the cathedrals of northern Europe. Since then, stained glass has been involved in a slow and steady decline, primarily because the artists and the craftsmen copied more and more the painters of the time and attempted to produce transparent paintings. In the process, they denied the very nature of the materials they were using.

Only the Art Nouveau era brought some serious innovations, changing the look and use of glass, since windows were made not only for churches but also for use in other types of environments. Much experimenting was done in the creation of the material itself, with the invention of different types of glass and new methods of assembling it.

But as a whole, and withstanding few notable exceptions, the world of the artist in stained glass and the craftsmen through the centuries partook only peripherally in the major art movements. Now and then an artist would become fascinated with glass and fall in love with its potential and bring to it a new taste, and a new attitude toward it.

Louis Comfort Tiffany was a painter before becoming interested in glass, and his interest spanned much beyond a specific medium; his mind and research suggest an interest in a whole way of being, and its aesthetics.

Contemporary Stained Glass

Since World War II, we have two basically different developments in the use of stained glass. During the reconstruction in Germany, a group of designers of stained glass, in close collaboration with architects, created a vast number of windows for churches and public buildings. The church authorities in Germany, unlike those elsewhere, were eager to rebuild their churches without going back to the past. They supported the growth and experiments that the new designers were undertaking. For the first time in centuries, the look and imprint of this work is not an attempt to nostalgically echo the achievements of another age, but rather to utilize the medium in a new and exciting way. Meistermann, Shaffrath and Johannes Schreiter have all used the medium—perhaps for the first time since the Gothic time—in its own right, copying nothing at all from the past. Glass becomes itself in their work, and is used in many environments effectively.

The other development is that stained glass has been used occasionally by artists who had made an imprint on the history of art outside the medium itself, and then would come to glass in one way or another and utilize it to their own ends. They bring to glass the whole flavor of their life and art experience.

Noteworthy are the windows of Matisse in the famous chapel at Vence in southern France. These windows are part of a whole environment, a masterpiece of simplicity and light use. Matisse designed not only the glass but also the doors, the sculptures, the beautiful drawings fired into the white tiles, and even the garments worn by the priests during the service.

Other works were designed by Rouault, Chagall, Leger, and others—and some are more successful than others. These artists bring to the medium so much from their whole life as painters, but the lack of thought given to the medium itself produces at times windows with a peculiar feel to them, such as Chagall's famous Jerusalem windows.

I find these windows most beautiful for their imagery, for the glass and the painting, yet to me it is inconceivable that Chagall himself did not design the lead line work, but left the task to Charles Marq. The lead lines in the windows scarcely relate or interplay with the images themselves. To me, the lead line work is a major means of expression unique to stained glass. To surrender the control of line placement is inconceivable.

The Environment

The most common problems of new-comers to the stained glass medium (including mature artists of other mediums) is their assumption that one can immediately create images and works without a direct and thorough experience of the properties and characteristics of the glass and lead themselves—without observing how the lead stretches, how the glass breaks, how the whole process feels before one creates major design.

Everything is possible if you can "think it." Perseverance and stubborn tenacity are of absolute importance through all the practical steps of a stained glass project, especially if the project is a "first," experimental in character, and requires facing problems for the first time. However, the ability to "think the unthinkable" is by far the most difficult ability to acquire and develop. The unthinkable is here all the time; we live in it. But it is difficult to divest ourselves of our cultural clothing and allow ourselves to lose our balance.

The drawings that follow are a plunge of mine, an attempt to redefine the use of glass in the environments in which we live. These drawings are meant to be understood as ideas, embryos, that can develop into many directions. They are an attempt to shed knowledge rather than accumulate more. Once you have absorbed and assimilated these images, this material, you should completely forget it, and go on thinking, dreaming, working.

"Art" is like a species of plant. It grows through time of its own volition; it creates itself in a way parallel to the process of evolution in Nature. But the soil of art is our very selves, and its roots draw mercilessly from our intellectual, emotional, and perceptual experiences. Glass and light in their love affair find their own way, and consume us on their path. Our eyes make them live; our minds make them grow. Allow yourself to surrender, live in accord with your heart and intuition, and die when they are spent. Light will find someone else.

These drawings are an invitation to architects to open up their spaces to intense perceptual delight, and suggest new ways to utilize the medium of stained glass in their buildings.

Every building has a character of its own, and only the real situation itself can suggest the windows appropriate to it. These designs are to be understood as a kind of "vocabulary of possibilities," ideas to pluck out, alter and apply appropriately somewhere else. I view the following drawings not as points of "arrival" but rather of "departure," an important understanding since the quality and originality of the environment where glass is placed is out of the glassmaker's hands.

Keep in mind that a building is the intersection of various realities. The first reality is the building's physical existence, its presence in our space as a sculpture, a shape. Another reality is its emotional importance to us who use it—we live, love, and work in such a space. Other realities may be pointed out but I wish to focus on the building as a place where light enters, travels and metamorphoses itself. Think of light, not of lighted walls, as the subject. Light might pour into a building with full force as direct sunlight but, as it approaches another area, it softens into a different quality by virtue of the shape of the environment. Light may almost

vanish into darkness until suddenly, by virtue of a light well, it's bright again. The journey of light and how it is perceived is what matters. Every building is a world defined by light. Thus the architect and the maker of glass must consciously define the quality of a given environment.

A stained glass window can have two kinds of presence in a space. A window may be small but extremely dense, a beautiful work in itself, a dot of intense light to set off like an accent, a counterpoint, a highlight, an entire somber wall.

Or glass may be present as an outgrowth of the walls, a more subtle but larger presence, a presence not overwhelming but rather sensitive, delicate. Such a window will not set off the architecture but be it. Such large areas

are also ideal for bringing into our lives the impersonal forces of Nature—tides, flood waters, the random scattered pebbles on the beach, a solid powerful rockface, a flame, a wall on fire (only for a concrete building! let it be no omen!). These images of Nature need not be violent, but may be as delicate as the feeling of spring coming, or the gentleness of the early morning of a fall day.

The following illustrations attempt to show the windows, their shapes and surfaces, in relation to the spaces they inhabit. I felt it important to point to this "relationship" rather than to the windows themselves, since these are just hinted at, rather than developed.

First, consider whether the shapes of your windows are appropriate. Must they be rectangles or squares? Windows next to each other in a series allow the possibility of a large single image flowing from one into the next, or the development of a theme with a variation in each window, or separate images in a series, as, for example, Dan Fenton's series in Chapter 5.

Light as an Intrinsic Component

These studies of direct sunlight through differently shaped apertures show the pattern the light creates on the floor or the walls as the sun travels from sunrise to sunset. This colored light, moving and bathing the room, is part of the piece itself. Becoming aware of this phenomenon in advance will make designing a window a much fuller experience, since not only the image is considered, but its effect on the environment.

1

1. Study of a shadow as it moves across the floor.
2. Study of light as it moves through a room.

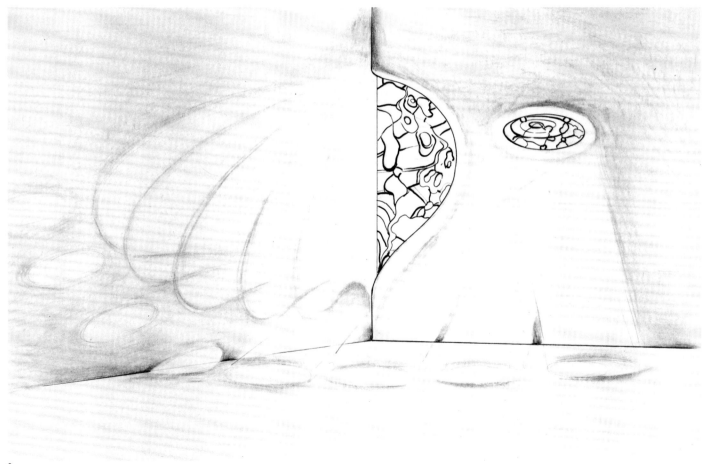

Windows in Rectangular Walls

Let us not always rely on the usual placement of windows on a rectangular wall! That straightforward arrangement has been used so many times. Differently shaped windows are shown on rectangular surfaces. Square or oval windows can be scattered in different ways on a wall surface to create an interesting effect. A waterfall tumbles from the corner of a room, and a creek winds down through a wall made of stone. A stream of lead lines flows, much like water, from one narrow rectangle to another. A leaf-shaped window breaks up a rectangular surface that I imagine in stucco.

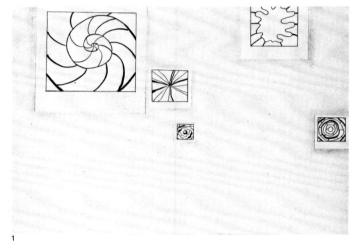

1

Studies for glass environments:
1. Study for placement of different-sized square windows on a rectangular wall.
2. Study for one image flowing through a series of rectangular tall windows.
3. Study for two sensuously shaped windows.
4. Study for a waterfall window.
5. Study for various oval apertures on a wall.
6. Study for glass in a stone wall, without geometric edges.

2

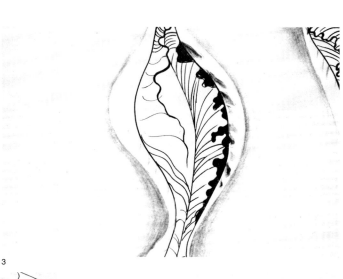

3

5

4

6

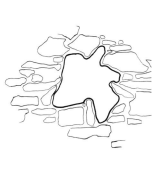

Windows on Nonflat Planes

Architects take notice! Stained glass
need not be used always on a flat surface. Walls can curve softly and the
glass can follow such a curve. Windows
can zigzag along such a wall, allowing
the viewer to see stained glass through
itself like a multiple overlay.

Corners and Ceilings

Why not? So rarely does stained glass
occupy a corner or even become part of
a ceiling: such a situation limits glass to
the role of a transparent painting. Used
in these ways, stained glass can cut
into the environment as a surprise.
Light pouring in from such an unusual
spot adds character to the space. If you
are in Carmel, California, don't fail to
see the baptistry of the All Saints' Epis-
copal Church. The stained glass is by
Mark Adams, built in Benicia by the
McKeever studio; the architecture is a
collaboration of Burde, Shaw and Associates. Stained glass cuts diagonally
through a wall, then takes in the ceiling
corner to become a skylight on the ceiling. Light enters the small baptistry
sideways, tints the walls marvelously.

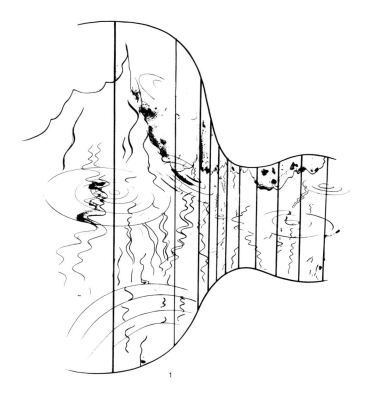

1

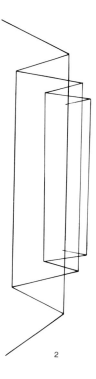

2

Stained glass on multiple planes:
1. Study for a curving glass wall.
2. Study for a zig-zag glass surface.
3. Two designs.
4. Plans for corner and ceiling.
5. Study for a band of glass across walls and ceiling.

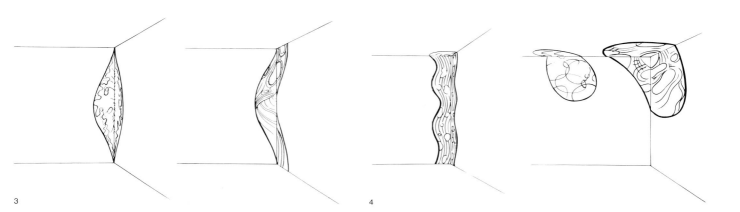

3

4

5

Surrealistic Windows

Unusual windows have a place if they are in the right context. With a bit of "pop" flavor, I designed a series of windows tucked under the ceiling of a curved space in a desert house. One detail shows a drop of water falling.

Mimicking Surrounding Materials

The ultimate decorative as well as humorous use of stained glass might be to extend the character and design of the materials enclosing the glass into the glass itself. Imagine a brick wall. It ends, but the brick-like shapes continue right into the glass of an aperture, perhaps a window, or a floor-to-ceiling aperture. The lead would become the cement, and the brown- and terracotta-colored glass the bricks! The effect would be that of a backlit brick wall. A window designed to look like a stone wall or a wood wall, with the glass painted or not, mimics and playfully makes a commentary on the materials the building is made of, extending them into light.

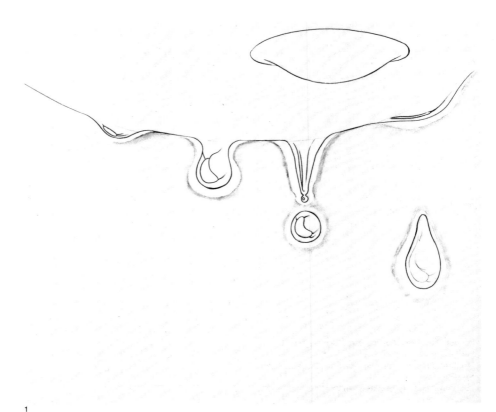

1

2

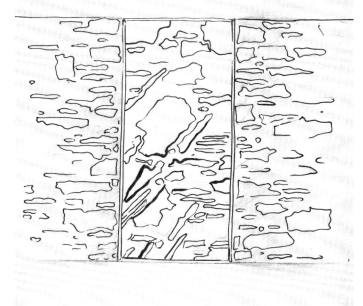

3

1. Glass water drop on ceiling, at curved wall
   juncture, and in wall.
2. Schematic study for brick wall pattern extended
   into glass.
3. Schematic study of stone wall pattern extended
   into glass.

Dome Glass

Stained glass has been assembled into domes and is beautiful used in this way. A dome is a mandala-like form; a mandala is the symbol of the effort to center, to encompass the totality of experience, to still time and the mind.

A placement of scattered ovals and circle openings in a wooden dome would create a set of cylindrical colored rays that would move across the floor throughout the day.

The second dome acts as a stream of glass which makes its way up to the very center-peak—an idea in homage to the Art Noveau epoch.

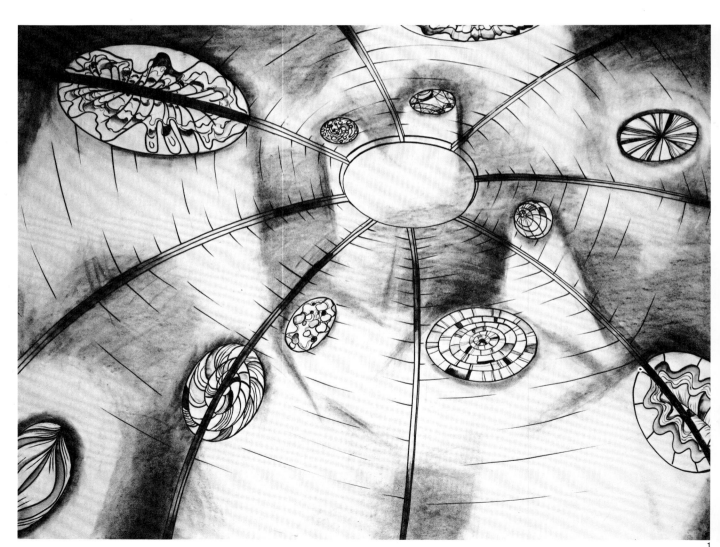

1

Good Situations for Stained Glass

The drawings I have done so far are schematic in character and show only the relationship between the glass apertures and the surfaces around them (rectangular walls, corners, and the like), but don't attempt to show how stained glass can enrich and relate to many different types of completed environments.

For this reason, I asked architect Lamberto Moris to seek out good typical situations in contemporary architectural structures where stained glass could be effective and meaningful.

These drawings are a result of our joint effort. Mr. Moris selected and rendered the environments and I designed the stained glass.

1. Sketch for a band of glass in the executive room of a skyscraper.
2. Sketch for a wave of glass in a skylight of college-type environment.
3. Sketch for glass in a large dome.

1

2

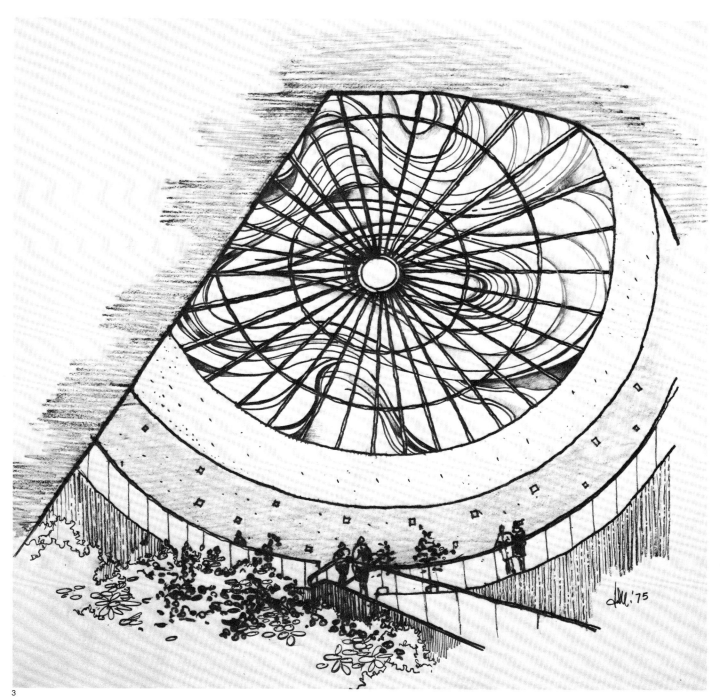

3

4

5

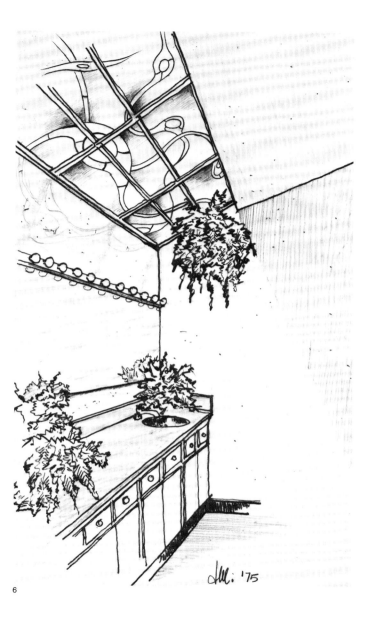

6

4. Sketch idea for waves of glass along a tunnel-like passageway.
5. Sketch for glass in A-frame window in private residence.
6. Sketch for bathroom skylight in residence.

Visionary Design Ideas

Consider the glass window in a wall: glistening eye, moist lips, a bleeding wound, the animating element of a wall: a gust of glass the sparkle, light, the movement, soul of a solid wall mass. Holes pierced in a thick wall or maybe the wall worn thin with its bare bones showing. Stained glass as the envelope; a veil, a jeweled shawl, a luminous carpet thrown over part of or an entire building..
—Paul Widess

I commissioned these few designs from Paul Widess, an architectural designer and builder, because I was moved and inspired by the free-flowing environments he has built in ferro cement. I most poignantly loved the feeling inside his spaces, with flowing curved walls and different textures here or there.

The spaces he creates are not built geometrically but organically. One feels himself in a cavern, rather than in a room. In such a space you feel poig-nantly the lack of sharp corners and angles; you feel instead that you are gently contained, since the forms of the environment echo those of nature.

His drawings suggest the complete merging of stained glass with the environment; the glass no longer is inserted into a wall, but becomes part of the wall itself. It grows on it or in it as a lichen on a rock.

1

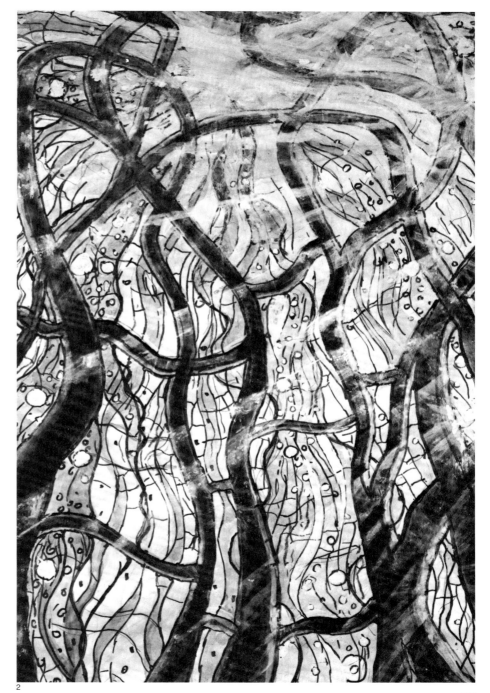

1. Idea sketch of an entire village with ferrocement glass towers.
2. Sketch of interior view of one of the towers.

2

3. Idea sketch for a hypothetical interior in ferrocement and glass.
4. Idea sketch for an entire building laced with
   stained glass.
5. Idea sketch for ferrocement house with glass
   on its apertures to the light.

3

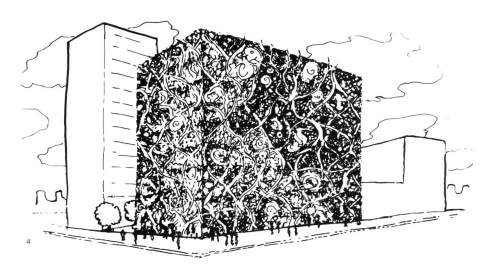

4

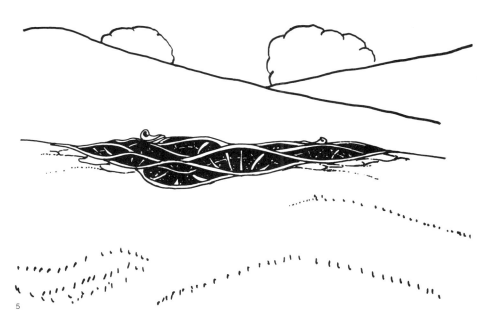

5

A Stained Glass Environment

A pool of water, made of mostly clear glass, goes from the far left to the extreme right of the building. The band of glass spans the entire front of the building and extends to one side. It is immediately above a magnificent view of the entrance to San Francisco's Golden Gate. For that reason, the glass is delicate so as not to press down on the airy landscape below it.

The series of twelve windows is tied together by the lead lines that define the ripples in the water, forming concentric ovals. These details describe "Reflection House," a stained glass environment in a San Francisco house designed by architect William Kirsch.

The surface of the water is viewed in perspective, the lead lines themselves define this perspective. The surface recedes and is broken up by the lines mostly vertical of the reflected plants wobbling and distorting on its surface. All the windows on the front of the house, which face north, are triangles and trapezoids; as we turn the corner to the east, the concluding window of the series is a rectangle. This window still contains the image of the surface of water reflecting plant forms, but, as a surprise, rocks appear beneath the surface and become visible through the clear body of water. The window's placement demanded the use of largely clear glass; I inserted intense color in the smaller triangles by using the images of flowers. These six flowers are interspersed throughout the whole front of the house, creating punctuation amid the flowing reflections of water. They are intensely colored and are viewed as closeups.

These windows were individually made with tender care; each window is a piece meant to stand alone, as well as to be part of the larger entity.

1

Reflection House, San Francisco:
1. Center detail of largest trapezoid window. (See p. 30.)

2

3

2. Interior view.
3. Interior view. (See p. 30.)

4. Interior view of corner. (See p. 29.)
5. Detail of westernmost four windows.
   (See p. 29.)

4

6

6. Detail of small flower in last window to west.

5

Introduction

I would like to devote this last chapter to the presentation of the works and ideas of five other stained glass artists who I profoundly respect and have learned much from. I feel a gratitude to each one for having shown me an approach to stained glass so different from my own.

Dan Fenton releases through his work a joyfulness and refreshing enthusiasm for stained glass.

Peter Mollica is very important for clearly expressing the fact that stained glass as a medium must be merged successfully with the architecture in which it is placed to become truly relevant.

Jeffrey Speeth (who collaborated with Inara Speeth in the design of many windows) I have met only once. His involvement with the medium has been a long one. In the ups and downs of his interesting career, he has accumulated a wealth of interesting and colorful experiences, and has produced many works that deal with unusual subject matter in glass—ranging from portraits of pop singers to a controversial series of erotic windows.

In the work of Paul Marioni I admire the incessant sense of humor, his keen awareness of the "absurd" which is involved in the making of anything at all, and his tenacity in experimentation. I admire his constant need to push the meaning and the technical limits of the medium one step further.

In Kathie Bunnell's work I admire the incredible care and sensitivity in each one of her windows, a care that so clearly expresses a reverence for the material itself, and for the subject matter.

Each of the five presents a statement of attitude toward their work and toward the medium of stained glass.

1. Kathie Bunnell, *Young Buckeye,* 1974, 28″ × 61½″.
2. Kathie Bunnell, *Moving through Darkness,* 1975, 36″ × 37″.

1

2

1

2

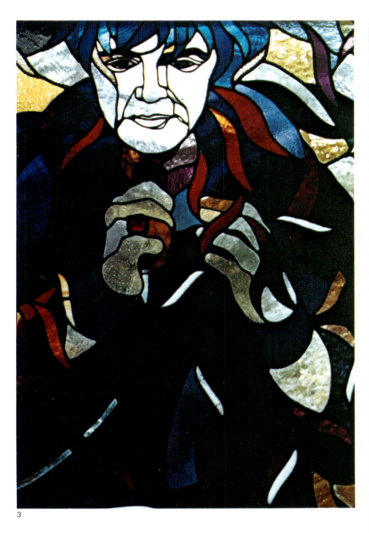

3

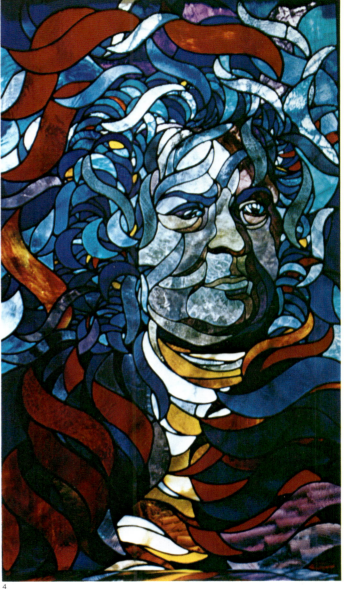

4

1. Paul Marioni, *Journey through the Valley of the Kings,* 1975, 24″×26″.
2. Paul Marioni, *Match Moderne,* 1973, 57″×30″.
3. Jeffrey Speeth, *Elvis,* detail of portraits of contemporary pop musicians, 1970-71.
4. Jeffrey Speeth, *Bach,* 1968, approximately 3½″×7″.

1. Peter Mollica, Berkeley residence, 1971,
   48″ × 60″.
2. Peter Mollica, *Green and White Squares*,
   1974, 20″ × 46″.
3. Dan Fenton, two panels from *Growth and
   Transformation*, 1972. Left panel, 15″ × 38″.
   Right panel, 15″ × 35″.

1

2

4

4. Dan Fenton, *Bass Notes*, 1974, 36″ × 72″.

Dan Fenton

Most of my work is in the format of the independent leaded glass panel. Although stained glass is primarily an architectural art, the autonomous panel format offers a much wider range of freedom in the exploration of the potential of glass (as a unique light-transmitting material), design imagery and artistic expression.

Much of the design imagery I use is derived from nature.

By studying the structure of living organisms, I have become aware of those elements of form that are present in all living things. I use these elements of form as a basic design theme that I work into an abstraction still containing the vitality of organic form. This way of designing stimulates me to feel color, to understand its qualities in transmitted light and to use it freely to create illusions of depth and space.

I am also influenced by music—contemporary improvisional jazz. Most of my recent work deals with the visual interpretation of structural concepts behind the music and the expression of the visions that play in my mind as I listen. I can feel a spacial dimension in music and see color in its sound.

Music will sometimes stimulate visions in my mind. The "Bass Notes" window is the result of one of those experiences. I awakened one morning to an Albert Ayler record playing on the stereo. In a state of semi-wakefulness I listened and drifted with it, seeing rhythmically pulsating layers of fire-like forms. The sounds from the bass stood out in a different way. They seemed to superimpose their form over the main flow and act as lenses that cooled and softened those fire-like forms that moved behind them.

On the conceptual level I perceive music not as it comes to my ears, note by note, but in the overall feeling derived from the composition as a whole. It is a transcendence from the time matrix in which musical sounds move and into the space dimension where you can see, hear and feel every element of a musical composition at once. It can be seen in its entirety or examined in part from any direction.

1

2

1. Dan Fenton, *The Passing of Migratory Sounds,*
   1972, 24″ × 36″.
2. Dan Fenton, *Light Rain,* 1974, 48″ × 54″.

3

4

3. Dan Fenton, *Seashell,* 1970, 20″ × 48″.
4-7. Dan Fenton, *Growth and Transformation,* 1972,
    38″ × 7′. The window and three details.

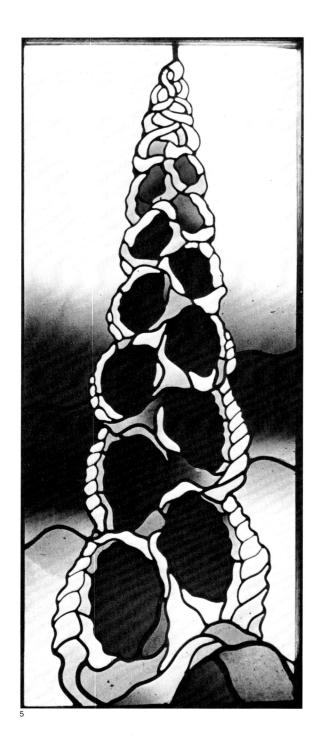

5

6

7

Peter Mollica

Most of the windows I've designed have been for private homes. It is challenging to design for homes, but I would like to design windows for churches or buildings of similar architectural form; that is, a large central room used primarily in daytime, in which the windows are designed as an integral part of the building. I am, at present, less interested in doing windows as paintings which stand alone as objects on/in a wall. I would eventually like to design the buildings, too, but in the next few years I would like to work closely with a few architects developing ways to make stained glass more architectural and in that way more effective.

Windows done for houses, other small rooms or art gallery shows of necessity tend to be focal points for visual entertainment. The proximity of the viewer makes it impossible for the window not to stand out and catch the eye, self-contained as a painting.

In larger spaces where they are seen at a distance, windows can be made to blend and become part of the walls around them and the building as a whole. I don't feel that stained glass has to act as a bright painting to be effective. The intensity of the colors in glass make them difficult to control and this lack of control is the major weakness of most of the windows being installed in architecture today. The temptation is to use all the power you have available to you, always a bad choice, in my opinion.

1

1. Peter Mollica, *Blue T,* 1972, 24″×36″.
2. Peter Mollica, untitled, 1971, 32″×56″.

2

3

3. Peter Mollica, untitled, 1971, 21″×61″.
4. Peter Mollica, *Chrome Bolt,* 1971, 12″×24″.

4

5

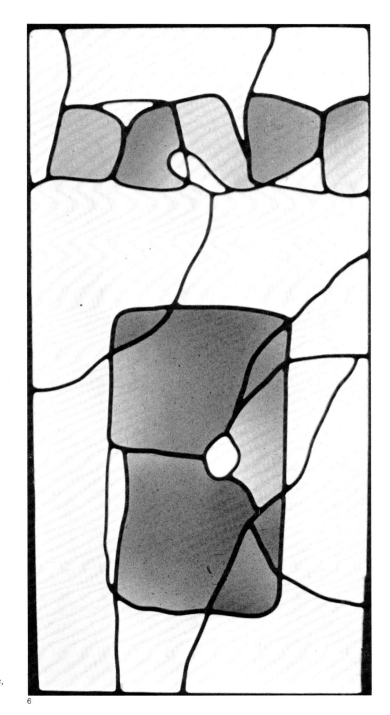

5. Peter Mollica, untitled,
   1972, 14″ × 25″.
6. Peter Mollica, *Schreiter's Blues,*
   1974, 18″ × 36″.

6

Jeffrey John Speeth

I've gone through a complete cycle in my thinking about glass.

I started pot-metal glazing professionally in 1961. I did several years of repair work, hundreds of windows. After a time, I decided that anything I did would be better than ninety-nine percent of the windows I was repairing. So, I just started making windows.

If there were no commissions, then I would make windows for myself. I'd buy old frames from a junk shop next door to my studio (in Cuyenga, California) and fill them up. I made a window a day for a long while.

My first four years were repair and prolificity: a self-served apprenticeship. I have only a few photos of what I did then, and I've recently started enjoying them.

Then, I started thinking—intellectualizing. I craved larger commissions that would take longer periods of time. I thought about simultaneous contrast (ancient glaziers' term: luminescence) to eradicate the lead line. I thought of color relationship, and Kandinsky moods. I began a liaison with an artist, and she induced more thought. I became obsessed and precious about my work.

I would recut pieces over and over again. My beeswax bill was enormous. There was even a period of time when I hated the color yellow. I gained prestige and lost money. My best friends were plastic sculptors. I started reading instead of looking at the pictures!

I have parted with the artist. I have moved to the country. And, I now believe, that, as Stalin said about literature, "Paper will put up with anything you put upon it." Colors can stand being next to each other. I no longer care if my windows turn to mud when you get sixty feet away from them. As a matter of fact, I think that's glorious.

I have a new partner who has brought back much of my earlier feelings about glass. He is Dan Head, and he was trained by a former student of mine, Dan Fenton of Oakland, California. He is the age I was when I started. He thinks nothing of the old-hat taboos. He'll gladly leave large, gaping holes in his work; and I have seen him work for days on a piece and then throw it out the window to crack it on the street below. "It needed cracking." We need each other to work and laugh. I feel a renewal of energy.

Now I reside in upper Appalachia. I am marrying a journalist-musician. I'll never feel challenged about the pure act of doing pot-metal work, again.

I enjoy everything I see in glass. And I like the stained glass contact paper you can put on your windows—I love the Japanese paper imitations of Tiffany-type shades.

There is no doubt in my mind that plastic eventually will replace stained glass. It already has, in many instances. The feeling of Bauhaus design is just one good example. Therefore, I believe that one should have fun, if one's days are numbered. I intend to have fun. My studio is an amusement park.

My style will be constant. There's nothing I can do about that. People who know glass will say, "That looks like a Speeth window." I shall simply exist in those stylized boundaries with total acceptance.

My next window for myself will be entitled, "My first window, by Jeffrey John Speeth, executed at the precocious age of six."

1. Jeffrey Speeth, portraits of contemporary pop
   musicians (first panel), 1970-71, approximately
   6½′ × 12′.

2

2. Jeffrey Speeth, portraits of contemporary pop
   musicians (second panel), 1970-71, approximately 6½′ × 12′. (See p. 195.)
3. Jeffrey Speeth, detail, portrait of contemporary
   pop musician.

4

4. Jeffrey Speeth, detail, portraits of contemporary pop musicians.
5. Jeffrey Speeth, detail, *Self Portrait*, 1965, 5' × 5'.

Paul Marioni

Some random thoughts—not necessarily in order. I'm constantly changing my mind. I got into glass because of Judy Raffael. She was the only one who had done something that didn't look like everything else. This gave me the notion that a lot of things hadn't been done in glass. It had been stuck in its traditions for a very long time. I can see now that when I started I really had no idea of its traditions. All glass looked alike, so I hadn't noticed it. I only knew what I wanted it to do and experimented with that. I continually do experiments (slumping, carving, breaking, painting, etc.), and I'm sure that this experimentation is what keeps my interest up. Often the unexpected results-—accidents—of a test prove to be blessings from the gods.

The amount of planning and the enormous number of labor hours executing a piece tend to be a severe drawback as my new ideas always make the present work somewhat of a distraction. Also I think stained glass artists (myself included) see it as serious business because of the work and thought that goes into it. I curse this and often think of quitting on windows in order to work more conceptually. Duchamp's "Fresh Window" carries this for me. The broken series I did recently came out of this. I wanted to work while visiting at Pilchuck so decided to break a whole wall of individual panes of glass to match the view outside the window with cracks in the windows. The first one I tried, I messed up and the whole pane of glass fell out. Terry Eaton was with me and asked me what the hell I was doing, breaking these windows while the owner wasn't at home. I realized that I didn't know, but felt good in the process. So I cut a replacement for that window and wrote the word NERVE in the glass with a cutter and tapped out the cracks to follow the word. Later I could see the frustration in having to rely on tools and glass and planning and all that goes with this serious business of stained glass. I wanted to work. I didn't want to be tied down to planning and equipment.

I can't get interested in all the "color and light" theories always floating around. I admire the strength of the current German stained glass but I think it relies too much on theory, or maybe it's the Americans who are working off of the Germans' theories that I have a hard time relating to. I think you have to be a salesman to have theories, you have to use your theories to sell your work. If you're working off a theory, you're expected to stick to it. It limits you, you start fitting your ideas to your theory, When I had the show at Nervo's (the broken series), Marvin Lipofsky (a prominent glassblower) thought it was a letdown and asked me when I was going to get back to work. "Let Tiffany Die" (a conceptual piece with lead draped over a string and broken glass underneath it) was meant to point out the very fact that traditions/expectations limit you.

Jeff Speeth's irreverant approach to subject matter relieves some of the boredom of the traditions of stained glass.

Glass is a challenging medium in many ways. It is inherently beautiful so that anything you do with it will nearly always be beautiful. Sometimes you can't get past this. Often I've seen a sheet of glass that by its own beauty inspired an idea. One of my students set out to do a grotesque window—it turned out to be beautiful (note: I feel this result was also largely due to the fact that she had tapped into herself). Glass also challenges because it is a cold hard medium. It is brittle. The fact that it breaks so easily reminds me of a man on a tightrope—always at the edge of losing it. It is probably for this reason that often little is done to the glass itself, such as slumping to shape it or painting and sandblasting to shade it or change the color.

1

1. Paul Marioni, *Luxury Liner,* 1972, 28¼″ × 30″.

2

3

2. Paul Marioni, *Auburn*, 1971, 24″ × 26″.
3. Paul Marioni, *Cadillac*, 1971, 28″ × 27″

4

5

4. Paul Marioni, *25 Years,* 1974, 28″×27″.
5. Paul Marioni, *The Lady in Waiting,* 1973,
   27½″×26″.

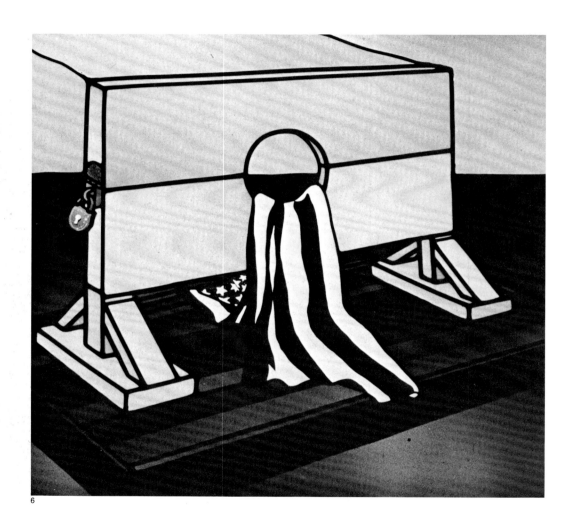

6

226

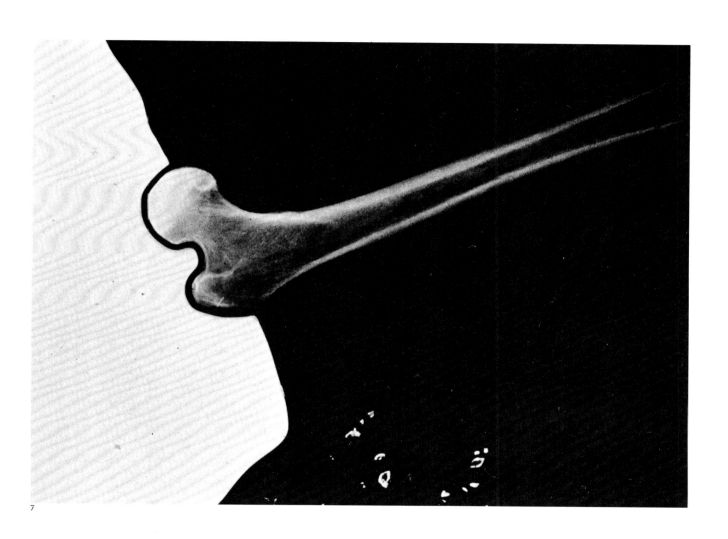

7

6. Paul Marioni, *Monetary Gair.,* 1973, 24″×26″.
7. Paul Marioni, *Metamorphose,* 1974, 21″×20″.

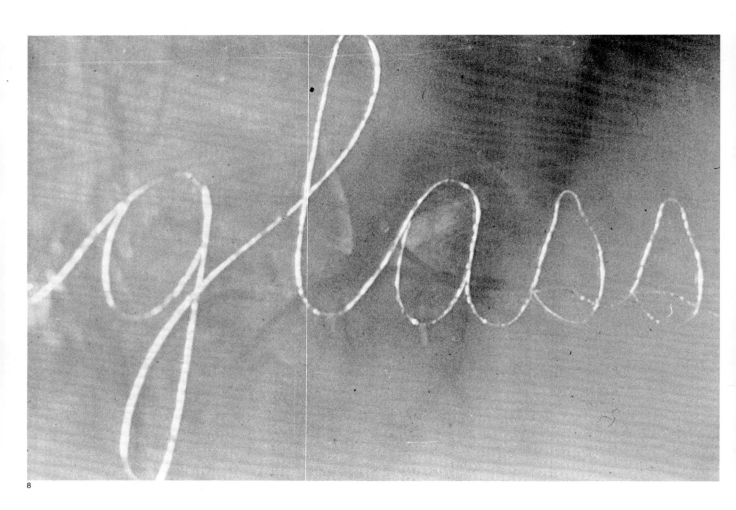

8

8. Paul Marioni, *Glass,* a light sketch from the
   Broken series, 1974, 18″×24″.
9. Paul Marioni, *Magritte,* 1973, 22″×20″.

The man in the white hat

10

10. Paul Marioni, *Dali*, 1972, 27½ × 26″.

Kathie Bunnell

My concern with interaction of color and the changing qualities of light led me from using watercolor to glass. The reasonings behind my using glass rather than another medium are many. They range from enjoying the sound of a clean snap when breaking a piece of glass to joy that comes through the discipline required to work with stained glass.

The nature of stained glass allows the artist a chance to create a suspended image in space which is luminous and transparent. Light changing as it passes through the stained glass gives the window life.

Stained glass also has great strength in the fact that color glowing and shedding light is jewel-like and pure. Hand blown and opalescent glasses carry traces of the active liquid state they were in before becoming flat sheets for use in windows. A sense of motion is inherent in glass. With stained glass, one looks at the already given sheet of glass for its expressive potential and uses it. A balance is always going on between the medium as guide and the will of the artist at work.

We are aware that color does not always stop at the edge of an object, say a purple flower in the forest. This purple shines beyond the edges of the petals and extends into the air around the petals. It's possible to achieve this kind of color phenomenon in glass.

I see windows as apertures or openings corollary to our eyes, ears, noses, mouths, pores, and the like. I feel that a stained glass window is an opening that bridges between worlds. As that, it should be freeing in a sensory way. A window is freeing to a room. Our eyes could be thought of as being to our skulls as windows are to a room.

I like to make windows that invite the viewer, that say, "You do the seeing." The window can be a door to inner worlds as well. In fact, I always think of windows in several ways. An invitation out into the garden, an invitation into the window, and an invitation into oneself—the viewer. The window becomes a bridge between all points.

We bring from ourselves dreams, images from the human psyche, glances out and back; these then are brought out to light. I think that a window need not be quiet or lulling but could be painful—in other words, difficult to confront.

Probing is the business of everyone —especially children and artists.

Glass is transparent to opaque in range. As a transparent, light-conducting medium, it offers a sense of revelation. Moments in one's life are transparent when they become filled with time—time present, time past, and time future. I like to try to express more than one time factor within a window. "Chain of Events" (19″ × 30″, September, 1974) is a window that involves more than one time sense. The antler is shed from the deer to take on a certain configuration.

The main involvement was a love for the weathering and changing of nature's matter. The antler has been shed. The shells are calcium houses for snails and then for the hermit crab. Someone has found them scattered across a beach by a series of motions that brought them in a rhythm of time and change to the beach. The man strung the shells to make a necklace. The woman put them on a deer antler. They sit there for awhile in a field of dark waves. So this is "Chain of Events."

The "Young Buckeye" window (28″ × 61½″, June, 1974, at the Green Gulch Zen Center in California) was drawn from life in February of 1974, and executed between March and June. I found the tree to be like a human body in my emotional experience of it. It's vertical as a spine. It expresses in the spiral growth of branches around its spine an URGE, pure urge, which is grace. Grace is gesture and all alive; things speak that way. "Buckeye" is a dancing body clothed in air. It has a center and around the center are spreading shapes of air like arms.

In "Moving Through Darkness" (36″ × 37″, January, 1975), I see the snake as rhythmic motion and his path as an arrow. He therefore holds in his head the obsidian arrowhead which he carries through an energized field of forces around him.

An idea emerged from this work which I call "pre-color." I define "pre-color" or "before-light" as color at its initial formation stage, as when the sun is just on the verge of coming up. It is almost felt as a delicate vibration as well as seen as such.

The Gothic work is powerful and beautiful; it has given to me and still does. But we have to shake off the preconception that a stained glass window has to be like the fourteenth, fifteenth, sixteenth century work, or like the later work of Tiffany. If we don't shake it off, we won't make space for now. I find, in my opinion, one good influence from the fact that stained glass has been from the church. I consider stained glass to be a religious medium and practice. "Religious" sounds to some rarified and very remote, but I think of religious experience as an attitude basic to life and a function, as is eating. It is a pleasure, besides.

My craftsmanship is careful because essentially the work is effecting me and is dedicated to the life I fully respect, and that can't be skimped on.

Being alive is taking chances and, as an artist, how do I know if what I make will last? If it lasts right now, reverberates and causes excitement, that is fine.

1. Kathie Bunnell, *Childhood Ikon,* 1975,
   27″ × 39½″.

2

3

2,3. Kathie Bunnell, *Chambered Nautilus*, 1972,
29″ × 56″.

4

5

4,5. Kathie Bunnell, *Passion Flower,* 1973,
    18″×23″: The window and detail.

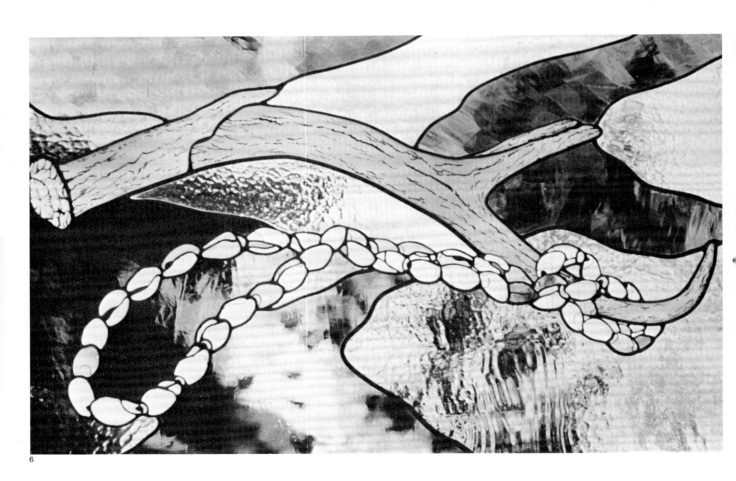

6

6. Kathie Bunnell, *Chain of Events,* 1974,
   30″×19″.
7. Kathie Bunnell, *Envisioning a Marriage,* 1975,
   37″×46″.

7

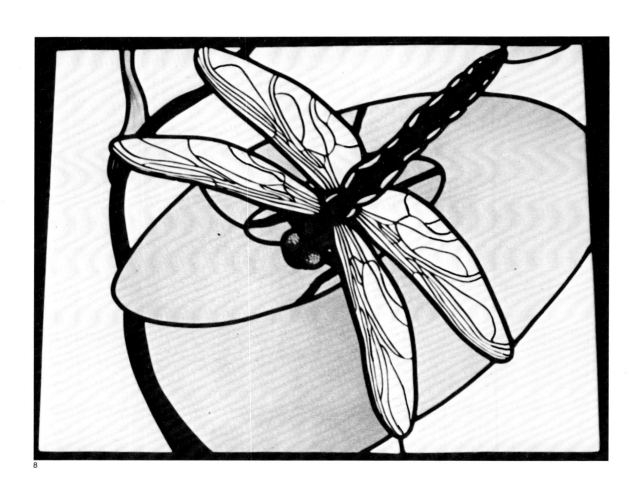

8

8. Kathie Bunnell, *Dragon-Fly*, 1972, 25″×21″.

Bibliography

Technique

E. Liddall Armitage, *Stained Glass: History, Technology and Practice,* Newton, Massachusetts: Charles T. Branford Co., 1959.

Jean Jacques Duval, *Working in Stained Glass,* New York: Thomas Y. Crowell Co., 1972.

Anita and Seymour Isenberg, *How to Work in Stained Glass,* New York: Chilton Book Co., 1972.

Lawrence Lee, *Stained Glass,* New York: Oxford University Press, 1967.

Robert and Gertrude Metcalf, *Making Stained Glass,* New York: McGraw-Hill Book Co., 1972.

Peter Mollica, *Stained Glass Primer,* Berkeley: Mollica Stained Glass Press, 1971.

Patrick Reyntiens Watson-Guptill, *Technique of Stained Glass,* New York: Guptill Publications, 1967.

Literary References

J. J. G. Alexander (introduction and legends), *Master of Mary of Burgunay, The Book of Hours for Englebert of Nassau,* Bodlian Library, Oxford, England, New York: George Braziller, 1970.

Carlos Castenada, *The Teachings of Don Juan: A Yaqui Way of Knowledge,* New York: Ballantine Books, 1969.
A Separate Reality: Further Conversations with Don Juan, New York: Touchstone/Simon and Schuster, 1971.
Journey to Ixtlan: The Lessons of Don Juan, New York: Touchstone/Simon and Schuster, 1972.
Tales of Power, New York: Simon and Schuster, 1974.

Herbert Marcuse, *Eros and Civilization: A Philosophical Inquiry into Freud,* New York: Vintage Books, 1962.

Shunryu Suzuki, *Zen Mind/Beginner's Mind,* New York and Tokyo: Weatherhill Book, 1970.

Contemporary Art, Design and Glass

Emilio Ambasz, Editor. *Italy, The New Domestic Landscape: Achievements and Problems of Italian Design,* New York: Museum of Modern Art, in collaboration with Centro di Florence, Italy, 1972.

John Baker & Alfred Lammer, *English Stained Glass,* New York: Harry N. Abrams, Inc. 1960.

Gregory Battock, Editor. *Idea Art: A Critical Anthology,* New York: E. P. Dutton and Co., Inc., 1973 (pb).
The New Art: A Critical Anthology, New York: E. P. Dutton and Co., Inc., 1966 (pb).

Albert Lewis, Editor. *Glass Art Magazine,* Glass Art Magazine, Inc., Box 7527, Oakland, California 94601.

Jean Leymarie, *The Jerusalem Windows of Marc Chagall,* New York: George Braziller, 1967.

Victor Papanek, *Design for the Real World: Human Ecology and Social Change,* New York: Pantheon Books (division of Random House), 1971.

John Piper, *Stained Glass: Art or Anti-Art,* New York: A Studio Vista/Reinhold art paperback (originally published in 1903).

Tom Wolfe, "The Painted Word: Modern Art Reaches the Vanishing Point," *Harper's Magazine,* April 1975.

Stained Glass and Architecture

Glass Art Magazine, Vol. 3, No. 5, October, 1975. This issue is devoted to the work of Ludwig Shaffrath.

Robert Sowers, *Stained Glass: An Architectural Art,* New York: University Books, Inc., 1965 (out of print).

Photography Credits

Dan Fenton 200, 201, 202, 203, 204, 205, 206, 215, 216, 217, 218, 219, 234, 235.
Charles Frizzell 29 right, 30 bottom, 31 top, 32 left, 186, 189, 208, 209, 210, 211, 212, 213.
Jack Fulton 221, 222, 223, 224, 225, 226, 229, 230.
Hans Halberstadt 20-21, 29 left, 30 top, 30 middle, 31 middle, 31 bottom, 32 right, 128, 130, 138, 185, 188, 190.
Bill Kane 26 left, 27, 60, 122 left, 127, 134, 135.
Paul Kunkel 227, 228.
Rita Mandelman 159.
Jean Myers 125 top.
Susan Shaw 146, 147, 148, 149, 150, 151, 152, 153, 154, 155, 156, 157, 158.
Peter Stackpole 236, 237, 238, 240.
Graham Waddill 5, 6.

All photographs not credited, including those on the cover and back cover, are by the author.

Note from the Publisher

I am interested in a new type of book production that grows out of the intimate relationship between publisher, author, designer, and editor.

My objective as a publisher is to produce a few fine books that grow out of my experiences in life. I care very much for those people who work with me using their various skills to make a reality of a book like *Stained Glass from Mind to Light*.

As a novice glassworker myself, I have felt a real need for a book such as this. My hope is that the book will prove to be as enriching an experience for you as it has been for those of us who helped create it, and that it will encourage you to be creative in your own way.

Ray Porter,
Mattole Press, San Francisco
March 1976